VIEUX CARRÉ

By TENNESSEE WILLIAMS

PLAYS

Baby Doll (a screenplay)
Camino Real
Cat on a Hot Tin Roof
Clothes for a Summer Hotel
Dragon Country
The Glass Menagerie
A Lovely Sunday for Creve Coeur
Small Craft Warnings
Stopped Rocking and Other Screenplays
A Streetcar Named Desire
Sweet Bird of Youth
THE THEATRE OF TENNESSEE WILLIAMS, VOLUME I
   Battle of Angels, A Streetcar Named Desire, The Glass Menagerie
THE THEATRE OF TENNESSEE WILLIAMS, VOLUME II
   The Eccentricities of a Nightingale, Summer and Smoke, The Rose Tattoo, Camino Real
THE THEATRE OF TENNESSEE WILLIAMS, VOLUME III
   Cat on a Hot Tin Roof, Orpheus Descending, Suddenly Last Summer
THE THEATRE OF TENNESSEE WILLIAMS, VOLUME IV
   Sweet Bird of Youth, Period of Adjustment, The Night of the Iguana
THE THEATRE OF TENNESSEE WILLIAMS, VOLUME V
   The Milk Train Doesn't Stop Here Anymore, Kingdom of Earth (The Seven Descents of Myrtle), Small Craft Warnings, The Two-Character Play
THE THEATRE OF TENNESSEE WILLIAMS, VOLUME VI
   27 Wagons Full of Cotton and Other Short Plays
THE THEATRE OF TENNESSEE WILLIAMS, VOLUME VII
   In the Bar of a Tokyo Hotel and Other Plays
27 Wagons Full of Cotton and Other Plays
The Two-Character Play
Vieux Carré

POETRY

Androgyne, Mon Amour
In the Winter of Cities

PROSE

Collected Stories
Eight Mortal Ladies Possessed
Hard Candy and Other Stories
The Knightly Quest and Other Stories
One Arm and Other Stories
The Roman Spring of Mrs. Stone
Where I Live: Selected Essays

VIEUX CARRÉ

by TENNESSEE WILLIAMS

A NEW DIRECTIONS BOOK

Manufactured in the United States of America

First published clothbound and as New Directions
Paperbook 482 in 1979

Published simultaneously in Canada by
Penguin Books Canada Limited

Library of Congress Cataloging in Publication Data

Williams, Tennessee, 1911-1983
Vieux carré
(A New Directions Book)
I. Title.
PS3545.I5365V5   1979   812'.5'4   78-26621
ISBN 0-8112-0727-7
ISBN 0-8112-0728-5 pbk.

New Directions Books are published for James Laughlin
by New Directions Publishing Corporation,
80 Eighth Avenue, New York 10011

FIFTH PRINTING

INSCRIBED TO KEITH HACK

VIEUX CARRÉ

STAGE SETTING FOR THE NOTTINGHAM PLAYHOUSE PRODUCTION BY VOYTEK

Photograph by John Vere Brown

The Nottingham Playhouse Production of *Vieux Carré* was presented at The Playhouse Theatre, Nottingham, on May 16, 1978 and at the Piccadilly Theatre, London, by Ian B. Albery for Calabash Productions Ltd., on August 9, 1978. It was directed by Keith Hack; stage design was by Voytek, lighting by Francis Reid, costumes by Maria Björnson, and music by Jeremy Nicholas; company stage manager, James Gill. The cast in order of appearance was as follows:

MRS. WIRE	SYLVIA MILES
NURSIE	NADIA CATTOUSE
THE WRITER	KARL JOHNSON
JANE	DI TREVIS
NIGHTINGALE	RICHARD KANE
MARY MAUDE	BETTY HARDY
MISS CARRIE	JUDITH FELLOWS
TYE	JONATHAN KENT
PHOTOGRAPHER	ROBIN McDONALD
SKY	JACK ELLIOTT

TIME: The period between winter 1938 and spring 1939.

PLACE: A rooming house, No. 722 Toulouse Street, in the French Quarter of New Orleans.

THE SETTING OF THE PLAY: The stage seems bare. Various playing areas may be distinguished by sketchy partitions and doorframes. In the barrenness there should be a poetic evocation of all the cheap rooming houses of the world. This one is in the Vieux Carré of New Orleans, where it remains standing, at 722 Toulouse Street, now converted to an art gallery. I will describe the building as it was when I rented an attic room in the late thirties, not as it will be designed, or realized for the stage.

It is a three-story building. There are a pair of alcoves, facing Toulouse Street. These alcove cubicles are separated by ply-wood, which provides a minimal separation (spatially) between the writer (myself those many years ago) and an older painter, a terribly wasted man, dying of tuberculosis, but fiercely denying this circumstance to himself.

A curved staircase ascends from the rear of a dark narrow passageway from the street entrance to the kitchen area. From there it ascends to the third floor, or gabled attic with its mansard roof.

A narrow hall separates the gabled cubicles from the studio (with skylight) which is occupied by Jane and Tye.

Obviously the elevations of these acting areas can be only suggested by a few shallow steps: a realistic setting is impossible, and the solution lies mainly in very skillful lighting and minimal furnishings.

PART ONE

WRITER [*spotlighted downstage*]: Once this house was alive, it was occupied once. In my recollection it still is but by shadowy occupants like ghosts. Now they enter the lighter areas of my memory.

[*Fade in dimly visible characters of the play, turning about in a stylized manner. The spotlight fades on the writer and is brought up on Mrs. Wire, who assumes her active character in the play.*]

MRS. WIRE: Nursie! Nursie—where's my pillows?

[*Nursie is spotlighted on a slightly higher level, looking up fearfully at something. She screams.*]

Hey, what the hell is going on in there!

NURSIE [*running down in a sort of football crouch*]: A bat, a bat's in the kitchen!

MRS. WIRE: Bat? I never seen a bat nowhere on these premises, Nursie.

NURSIE: Why, Mizz Wire, I swear it was a bull bat up there in the kitchen. You tell me no bats, why, they's a pack of bats that hang upside down from that ole banana tree in the court-yard from dark till daybreak, when they all scream at once and fly up like a—explosion of—damned souls out of a graveyard.

MRS. WIRE: If such a thing was true—

NURSIE: As God's word is true!

5

MRS. WIRE: I repeat, if such a thing was true—which it isn't—an' you go tawkin' about it with you big black mouth, why it could ruin the reputation of this rooming house which is the only respectable rooming house in the Quarter. Now where's my pillows, Nursie?

NURSIE [sotto voce *as she arranges the pallet*]: Shit . . .

MRS. WIRE: What you say?

NURSIE: I said shoot . . . faw shit. You'd see they're on the cot if you had a light bulb in this hall. [*She is making up the cot.*] What you got against light? First thing God said on the first day of creation was, "Let there be light."

MRS. WIRE: You hear him say that?

NURSIE: You never read the scriptures.

MRS. WIRE: Why should I bother to read 'em with you quotin' 'em to me like a female preacher. Book say this, say that, makes me sick of the book. Where's my flashlight, Nursie?

NURSIE: 'Sunder the pillows. [*She stumbles on a heavy knapsack.*] Lawd! What that there?

MRS. WIRE: Some crazy young man come here wantin' a room. I told him I had no vacancies for Bourbon Street bums. He dropped that sack on the floor and said he'd pick it up tomorrow, which he won't unless he pays fifty cents for storage . . .

NURSIE: It's got something written on it that shines in the dark.

MRS. WIRE: "Sky"—say that's his name. Carry it on upstairs with you, Nursie.

6

NURSIE: Mizz Wire, I cain't hardly get myself up them steps no more, you know that.

MRS. WIRE: Shoot.

NURSIE: Mizz Wire, I think I oughta inform you I'm thinkin' of retirin'.

MRS. WIRE: *Retirin'* to what, Nursie? The banana tree in the courtyard with the bats you got in your head?

NURSIE: They's lots of folks my age, black an' white, that's called bag people. They just wander round with paper bags that hold ev'rything they possess or they can collect. Nights they sleep on doorsteps: spend days on boxes on corners of Canal Street with a tin cup. They get along: they live—long as intended to by the Lord.

MRS. WIRE: Yor place is with me, Nursie. √

NURSIE: I can't please you no more. You keep callin' Nursie, √ Nursie, do this, do that, with all these stairs in the house and my failin' eyesight. No Ma'am, it's time for me to retire.

[*She crosses upstage. The kitchen area is dimly lighted. Nursie sits at the table with a cup of chicory coffee, eyes large and ominously dark as the continent of her race.*

[*A spot of light picks up the writer dimly at the entrance to the hall.*]

MRS. WIRE: Who? Who?

WRITER: It's—

MRS. WIRE: *You* . . .

WRITER: Mrs. Wire, you're blinding me with that light. [*He shields his left eye with a hand.*]

MRS. WIRE [*switching off the light*]: Git upstairs, boy. We'll talk in the mawnin' about your future plans.

WRITER: I have no plans for the future, Mrs. Wire.

MRS. WIRE: That's a situation you'd better correct right quick.

[*The writer, too, collides with the bizarre, colorfully decorated knapsack.*]

WRITER: What's—?

MRS. WIRE: Carry that sack upstairs with you. Nursie refused to.

[*With an effort the writer shoulders the sack and mounts a step or two to the kitchen level.*]

WRITER: Mrs. Wire told me to carry this sack up here.

NURSIE: Just put it somewhere it won't trip me up.

WRITER: Sky? Sky?

NURSIE: She say that's his name. Whose name? I think her mind is goin' on her again. Lately she calls out, "Timmy, Timmy," or she carries on conversations with her dead husband, Horace . . .

WRITER: A name—Sky? [*To himself.*] Shines like a prediction.

[*He drops the knapsack at the edge of the kitchen light and wanders musingly back to the table. Nursie automatically pours him a cup of chicory.*

[*Again the area serving as the entrance passage is lighted, and the sound of a key scraping at a resistant lock is heard.*]

MRS. WIRE [*starting up from her cot*]: Who? Who?

[*Jane enters exhaustedly.*]

JANE: Why, Mrs. Wire, you scared me! [*She has an elegance about her and a vulnerability.*]

MRS. WIRE: Miss Sparks, what're you doin' out so late on the streets of the Quarter?

JANE: Mrs. Wire, according to the luminous dial on my watch, it is only ten after twelve.

MRS. WIRE: When I give you a room here . . .

JANE: Gave me? I thought rented . . .

MRS. WIRE [*cutting through*]: I told you a single girl was expected in at midnight.

JANE: I'm afraid I didn't take that too seriously. Not since I lived with my parents in New Rochelle, New York, before I went to college, have I been told to be in at a certain hour, and even then I had my own key and disregarded the order more often than not. However! I *am* going to tell you why and where I've gone tonight. I have gone to the all-night drugstore, Waterbury's, on Canal Street, to buy a spray can of Black Flag, which is an insect repellent. I took a cab there tonight and made this purchase because, Mrs. Wire, when I opened the window without a screen in my room, a cockroach, a *flying* cockroach, flew right into my face and was followed by a squadron of others. *Well!* I do *not* have an Oriental, a Buddhistic tolerance for certain insects, least of all a cockroach and even less a flying one. Oh, I've learned to live reluctantly with the ordinary pedestrian kind of cockroach, but to have one fly directly into my face almost gave me convulsions! Now as for the window without a screen, if a screen has not been put in that window by tomorrow, I will buy one for it myself and deduct the cost from next month's rent. [*She goes past Mrs. Wire toward the steps.*]

MRS. WIRE: Hold on a minute, young lady. When you took your room here, you gave your name as Miss Sparks. Now is that young fellow that's living up there with you Mr. Sparks, and if so why did you register as Miss instead of Mrs.?

JANE: I'm sure you've known for some time that I'm sharing my room with a young man, whose name is not Mr. Sparks, whose name is Tye McCool. And if that offends your moral scruples—well—sometimes it offends mine, too.

MRS. WIRE: If I had not been a young lady myself once! Oh yes, once, yaiss! I'd have evicted both so fast you'd think that . . .

JANE: No, I've stopped thinking. Just let things happen to me.

[*Jane is now at the stairs and starts up them weakly. Mrs. Wire grunts despairingly and falls back to her cot. Jane enters the kitchen.*]

NURSIE: Why, hello, Miss Sparks.

JANE: Good evening, Nursie—why is Mrs. Wire sleeping in the entrance hall?

NURSIE: Lawd, that woman, she got the idea that 722 Tou-

louse Street is the address of a jailhouse. And she's the keeper—
have some hot chick'ry with me?

JANE: Do you know I still don't know what chicory is? A
beverage of some kind?

NURSIE: Why chicory's South'n style coffee.

JANE: Oh, well, thank you, maybe I could try a bit of it to
get me up that flight of stairs . . .

[*She sits at the table. Below, the door has opened a third time.
The painter called Nightingale stands in the doorway with
a pickup.*]

MRS. WIRE: Who? Ah!

NIGHTINGALE [*voice rising*]: Well, cousin, uh, Jake . . .

PICKUP [*uneasily*]: Blake.

NIGHTINGALE: Yes, we do have a lot of family news to exchange. Come on in. We'll talk a bit more in my room.

MRS. WIRE: In a pig's snout you will!

NIGHTINGALE: Why, Mrs. Wire! [*He chuckles, coughs.*] Are
you sleeping in the hall now?

MRS. WIRE: I'm keeping watch on the comings and goings at
night of tenants in my house.

NIGHTINGALE: Oh, yes, I know your aversion to visitors at
night, but this is my first cousin. I just bumped into him at Gray
Goose bus station. He is here for one day only, so I have taken

11

the license of inviting him in for a little family talk since we'll have no other chance.

MRS. WIRE: If you had half the cousins you claim to have, you'd belong to the biggest family since Adam's.

PICKUP: Thanks, but I got to move on. Been nice seeing you—cousin . . .

NIGHTINGALE: Wait—here—take this five. Go to the America Hotel on Exchange Alley just off Canal Street, and I will drop in at noon tomorrow—cousin . . . [*He starts to cough.*]

PICKUP: Thanks, I'll see ya, cousin.

MRS. WIRE: Hah, cousin.

[*Nightingale coughs and spits near her cot.*]

Don't you spit by my bed!

NIGHTINGALE: Fuck off, you old witch!

MR. WIRE: What did you say to me?

NIGHTINGALE: Nothing not said to and about you before! [*He mounts the steps.*]

MRS. WIRE: Nursie! Nursie! [*Receiving no response she lowers herself with a groan onto the cot.*]

NIGHTINGALE [*starting up the stairs*]: Midnight staircase—still in—your [*coughs*] fatal position . . . [*He climbs slowly up.*]

[*The writer, Jane, and Nursie are in the kitchen. The crones*

12

enter, wild-eyed and panting with greasy paper bags. The kitchen area is lighted.]

MARY MAUDE: Nursie? Miss Carrie and I ordered a little more dinner this evening than we could eat, so we had the waiter put the remains of the, the—

MISS CARRIE [*her wild eyes very wild*]: The steak "Diane," I had the steak Diane and Mary Maude had the chicken "bonne femme." But our eyes were a little bigger than our stomachs.

MARY MAUDE: The sight of too much on a table can kill your appetite! But this food is too good to waste.

MISS CARRIE: And we don't have ice to preserve it in our room, so would you kindly put it in Mrs. Wire's icebox, Nursie.

NURSIE: The last time I done that Miss Wire raised Cain about it, had me throw it right out. She said it didn' smell good.

JANE: I have an icebox in which I'd be glad to keep it for you ladies.

MARY MAUDE: Oh, that's very kind of you!

WRITER [*rising from the kitchen table*]: Let me carry it up.

[*He picks up the greasy bags and starts upstairs. Miss Carrie's asthmatic respiration has steadily increased. She staggers with a breathless laugh.*]

MARY MAUDE: Oh, Miss Carrie, you better get right to bed. She's having another attack of her awful asthma. Our room gets no sun, and the walls are so damp, so—dark . . .

[*They totter out of the light together.*]

13

NURSIE [*averting her face from the bag with a sniff of repugnance*]: They didn't go to no restaurant. They been to the garbage pail on the walk outside, don't bother with it, it's spoiled [*pointing upstage*] just put it over there, I'll throw it out.

JANE: I wonder if they'd be offended if I bought them a sack of groceries at Solari's tomorrow.

NURSIE: Offend 'em did you say?

JANE: I meant their pride.

NURSIE: Honey, they gone as far past pride as they gone past mistaking a buzzard for a bluebird.

[*She chuckles. Tye appears. Jane pretends not to notice.*]

JANE: I'm afraid pride's an easy thing to go past sometimes. I am living—I am sharing my studio with a, an addicted—delinquent, a barker at a—stripshow joint. [*She has pretended to ignore Tye's disheveled, drugged, but vulnerably boyish appearance at the edge of the light.*]

TYE [*in a slurred voice*]: You wouldn't be tawkin' about—nobody—present . . .

JANE: Why, hello, Tye. How'd you get back so early? How'd you get back at all, in this—condition?

TYE: Honey! If I didn't have my arms full of—packages.

JANE: The less you say out loud about the hot merchandise you've been accumulating here . . .

TYE: Babe, you're asking for a— [*He doubles his fist.*]

14

JANE: Which I'd return with a kick in the balls! [*She gasps.*] My Lord, did I say that?

MRS. WIRE: What's that shoutin' about?

[*Jane breaks into tears. She falls back into the chair and buries her head in her arms.*]

TYE: Hey, love, come here, I knocked off work early to be with you—do you think I'd really hit you?

JANE: I don't know . . .

TYE: Come to—bed . . .

JANE: Don't lean on me.

[*They cross out of the light. The writer looks after them wistfully as the light dims out.*]

The writer has undressed and is in bed. Nightingale coughs—a fiendish, racking cough. He is hacking and spitting up bloody phlegm. He enters his cubicle.

Then across the makeshift partition in the writer's cubicle, unlighted except by a faint glow in its alcove window, another sound commences—a sound of dry and desperate sobbing which sounds as though nothing in the world could ever appease the wound from which it comes: loneliness, inborn and inbred to the bone.

Slowly, as his coughing fit subsides, Nightingale, the quick-sketch artist, turns his head in profile to the sound of the sobbing. Then the writer, across the partition, is dimly lighted, too. He is also sitting up on his cot, staring at the partition between his cell and Nightingale's.

Nightingale clears his throat loudly and sings hoarsely and softly a pop song of the era such as "If I Didn't Care" or "Paper Doll." Slowly the audience of one whom he is serenading succeeds in completely stifling the dry sobbing with a pillow. Nightingale's voice rises a bit as he gets up and lights a cigarette; then he goes toward the upstage limit of the dim stage lighting and makes the gesture of opening a door.

He moves into the other gable room of the attic and stands, silent, for several beats of the song as the writer slowly, reluctantly, turns on his cot to face him.

NIGHTINGALE: . . . I want to ask you something.

WRITER: Huh?

NIGHTINGALE: The word "landlady" as applied to Mrs. Wire and to all landladies that I've encountered in my life—isn't it the biggest one-word contradiction in the English language? [*The writer is embarrassed by Nightingale's intrusion and steady scrutiny.*] She owns the land, yes, but is the witch a lady? Mind if I switch on your light?

WRITER: The bulb's burned out.

NIGHTINGALE [*chuckles and coughs*]: She hasn't replaced a burnt-out light bulb in this attic since I moved here last spring. I have to provide my own light bulbs by unscrewing them from the gentleman's lavatory at the City of the Two Parrots, where I ply my trade. Temporarily, you know. Doing portraits in pastel of the tourist clientele. [*His voice is curiously soft and intimate, more as if he were speaking of personal matters.*]

Of course I . . . [*He coughs and clears his throat.*] . . . have no shame about it, no guilt at all, since what I do there is a travesty of my talent, I mean a prostitution of it, I mean, painting these tourists at the Two Parrots, which are actually two very noisy macaws. Oh, they have a nice patio there, you know, palm trees and azaleas when in season, but the cuisine and the service . . . abominable. The menu sometimes includes cockroaches . . . (There are a lot of great eating places in New Orleans, like Galatoire's, Antoine's, Arnaud's in the Vieux Carré and . . . Commander's Palace and Plantation House in the Garden District . . . lovely old mansions, you know, converted to restaurants with a gracious style . . . haunted by dead residents, of course, but with charm . . .)

[*This monologue is like a soothing incantation, interspersed with hoarseness and coughing.*]

Like many writers, I know you're a writer, you're a young man of very few spoken words, compared to my garrulity.

WRITER: Yes, I . . .

NIGHTINGALE: So far, kid, you're practically . . . monosyllabic.

WRITER: I . . . don't feel well . . . tonight.

NIGHTINGALE: That's why I intruded. You have a candle on that box beside your cot.

WRITER: Yes, but no matches.

NIGHTINGALE: I have matches, I'll light it. Talk is easier . . . [*He strikes the match and advances to the writer's bedside.*] . . . between two people visible to each other, if . . . not too sharply . . . [*He lights the candle.*] Once I put up for a night in a flophouse without doors, and a gentleman entered my cubicle without invitation, came straight to my cot and struck a match, leaned over me peering directly into my face . . . and then said, "No," and walked out . . . as if he assumed that I would have said, "Yes." [*He laughs and coughs.*]

[*Pause*]

You're not a man of few words but a boy of no words. I'll just sit on the cot if you don't object.

WRITER: . . . I, uh . . . do need sleep.

NIGHTINGALE: You need some company first. I know the sound of loneliness, heard it through the partition. [*He has sat on the cot. The writer huddles away to the wall, acutely embarrassed.*] . . . Trying not to, but crying . . . why try not to? Think it's unmanly? Crying is a release for man or woman . . .

WRITER: I was taught not to cry because it's . . . humiliating . . .

NIGHTINGALE: You're a victim of conventional teaching, which you'd better forget. What were you crying about? Some particular sorrow or . . . for the human condition.

WRITER: Some . . . particular sorrow. My closest relative died last month.

NIGHTINGALE: Your mother?

WRITER: The mother of my mother, Grand. She died after a long illness just before I left home, and at night I remember . . .

NIGHTINGALE [*giving a comforting pat*]: Well, losses must be accepted and survived. How strange it is that we've occupied these adjoining rooms for about three weeks now and have just barely said hello to each other when passing on the stairs. You have interesting eyes.

WRITER: In what way do you mean?

NIGHTINGALE: Isn't the pupil of the left one a little bit lighter?

WRITER: . . . I'm afraid I'm . . . developing a—cataract in that eye.

NIGHTINGALE: That's not possible for a kid.

WRITER: I am twenty-eight.

NIGHTINGALE: What I meant is, your face is still youthful as your vulnerable nature, they go—together. Of course, I'd see an oculist if you suspect there's a cataract.

WRITER: I plan to when I . . . if I . . . can ever afford to . . . the vision in that eye's getting cloudy.

NIGHTINGALE: Don't wait till you can afford to. Go straight away and don't receive the bill.

WRITER: I couldn't do that.

NIGHTINGALE: Don't be so honest in this dishonest world. [*He pauses and coughs.*] Shit, the witch don't sleep in her bedroom you know.

WRITER: Yes, I noticed she is sleeping on a cot in the hall now.

NIGHTINGALE: When I came in now she sprang up and hollered out, "Who?" And I answered her with a hoot owl imitation, "Hoo, Hooo, Hooooo." Why, the lady is all three furies in one. A single man needs visitors at night. Necessary as bread, as blood in the body. Why, there's a saying, "Better to live with your worst enemy than to live alone."

WRITER: Yes, loneliness is an—affliction.

NIGHTINGALE: Well, now you have a friend here.

WRITER [*dryly*]: Thanks.

NIGHTINGALE: Of course we're in a madhouse. I wouldn't tolerate the conditions here if the season wasn't so slow that—my financial condition is difficult right now. I don't like insults and *la vie solitaire*—with bedbugs bleeding me like leeches . . . but now we know each other, the plywood partition between us has been dissolved, no more just hellos. So tonight you were crying in here alone. What of it? Don't we all? Have a cigarette.

WRITER: Thanks.

[*Nightingale holds the candle out.*]

I won't smoke it now, I'll save it till morning. I like a cigarette when I sit down to work.

[*Nightingale's steady scrutiny embarrasses him. They fall silent. After several beats, the writer resumes.*]

There's—a lot of human material—in the Quarter for a writer . . .

NIGHTINGALE: I used to hear you typing. Where's your typewriter?

WRITER: I, uh, hocked it.

NIGHTINGALE: That's what I figured. Wha'd you get for it?

WRITER: Ten dollars. It was a secondhand Underwood portable. I'm worried about just how I'll redeem it. [*He is increasingly embarrassed.*]

NIGHTINGALE: Excuse my curiosity, I mean concern. It's sympathetic . . . smoke a cigarette now and have another for' mawnin'. You're not managing right. Need advice and . . . company in this sad ole house. I'm happy to give both if accepted.

WRITER: . . . I appreciate . . . both.

NIGHTINGALE: You don't seem experienced yet . . . kid, are you . . . excuse my blunt approach . . . but are you . . . ? [*He completes the question by placing a shaky hand on the writer's crumpled, sheet-covered body.*]

WRITER [*in a stifled voice*]: Oh . . . I'm not sure I know . . . I . . .

NIGHTINGALE: Ain't come out completely, as we put it?

WRITER: Completely, no, just one—experience.

NIGHTINGALE: Tell me about that one experience.

WRITER: I'm not sure I want to discuss it.

NIGHTINGALE: That's no way to begin a confidential friendship.

WRITER: . . . Well, New Year's Eve, I was entertained by a married couple I had a letter of introduction to when I came down here, the . . . man's a painter, does popular bayou pictures displayed in shop windows in the Quarter, his name is . . .

NIGHTINGALE: Oh, I know him. He's got a good thing going, commercially speaking, tourists buy them calendar illustrations in dreamy rainbow colors that never existed but in the head of a hack like him.

WRITER: . . . The, uh, atmosphere is . . . effective.

NIGHTINGALE: Oh, they sell to people that don't know paint from art. Maybe you've never seen artistic paintings. [*His voice shakes with feverish pride.*] I could do it, in fact I've done good painting, serious work. But I got to live, and you can't live on good painting until you're dead, or nearly. So, I make it, temporarily, as a quick sketch artist. I flatter old bitches by makin' 'em ten pounds lighter and ten years younger and with some touches of—decent humanity in their eyes that God forgot to put there, or they've decided to dispense with, not always easy. But what is? So—you had an experience with the bayou painter? I didn't know he was, oh, inclined to boys, this is killing.

WRITER [*slowly with embarrassment*]: It wasn't with Mr. Block, it was with a . . . paratrooper.

NIGHTINGALE: Aha, a paratrooper dropped out of the sky for you, huh? You have such nice smooth skin . . . Would you like a bit of white port? I keep a half pint by my bed to wash down my sandman special when this touch of flu and the bedbugs keep me awake. Just a mo', I'll fetch it, we'll have a nightcap—now that we're acquainted! [*He goes out rapidly, coughing, then rushes back in with the bottle.*]

The witch has removed the glass, we'll have to drink from the bottle. I'll wash my pill down now, the rest is yours. [*He pops a capsule into his mouth and gulps from the bottle, immediately coughing and gagging. He extends the bottle to the writer.*

[*Pause. The writer half extends his hand toward the bottle, then draws it back and shakes his head.*]

Oh yes, flu is contagious, how stupid of me, I'm sorry.

WRITER: Never mind, I don't care much for liquor.

NIGHTINGALE: Where you from?

WRITER: . . . St. Louis.

NIGHTINGALE: Christ, do people live there?

WRITER: It has a good art museum and a fine symphony orchestra and . . .

NIGHTINGALE: No decent gay life at all? ✓

WRITER: You mean . . .

NIGHTINGALE: You know what I mean. I mean like the . . . paratrooper.

WRITER: Oh. No. There could be but . . . living at home . . .

NIGHTINGALE: Tell me, how did it go with the paratrooper who descended on you at Block's?

WRITER: Well at midnight we went out on the gallery and he, the paratrooper, was out on the lower gallery with a party of older men, antique dealers, they were all singing "Auld Lang Syne."

23

NIGHTINGALE: How imaginative and *appropriate* to them.

WRITER: —I noticed him down there and he noticed me.

NIGHTINGALE: Noticing him?

WRITER: . . . Yes. He grinned, and hollered to come down; he took me into the lower apartment. It was vacant, the others still on the gallery, you see I . . . couldn't understand his presence among the . . .

NIGHTINGALE: Screaming old faggots at that antique dealer's. Well, they're rich and they buy boys, but that's a scene that you haven't learned yet. So. What happened downstairs?

WRITER: He took me into a bedroom; he told me I looked pale and wouldn't I like a sunlamp treatment. I thought he meant my face so I—agreed—

NIGHTINGALE: Jesus, you've got to be joking.

WRITER: I was shaking violently like I was a victim of—St. Vitus's Dance, you know, when he said, "Undress"!

NIGHTINGALE: But you did.

WRITER: Yes. He helped me. And I stretched out on the bed under the sunlamp and suddenly he—

NIGHTINGALE: . . . turned it off and did you?

WRITER: Yes, that's what happened. I think that he was shocked by my reaction.

NIGHTINGALE: You did *him* or—?

WRITER: . . . I told him that I . . . loved . . . him. I'd been drinking.

NIGHTINGALE: Love can happen like that. For one night only.

WRITER: He said, he laughed and said, "Forget it. I'm flying out tomorrow for training base."

NIGHTINGALE: He said to you, "Forget it," but you didn't forget it.

WRITER: No . . . I don't even have his address and I've forgotten his name . . .

NIGHTINGALE: Still, I think you loved him.

WRITER: . . . Yes. I . . . I'd like to see some of your serious paintings sometime.

NIGHTINGALE: Yeah. You will. Soon. When I get them canvases shipped down from Baton Rouge next week. But meanwhile . . . [*His hand is sliding down the sheet.*] How about this?

WRITER [*with gathering panic*]: . . . I think I'd better get some sleep now. I didn't mean to tell you all that. Goodnight, I'm going to sleep.

NIGHTINGALE [*urgently*]: This would help you.

WRITER: I need to sleep nights—to work.

NIGHTINGALE: You are alone in the world, and I am, too. Listen. Rain!

[*They are silent. The sound of rain is heard on the roof.*]

25

Look. I'll give you two things for sleep. First, this. [*He draws back the sheet. The light dims.*] And then one of these pills I call my sandman special.

WRITER: I don't . . .

NIGHTINGALE: Shh, walls have ears! Lie back and imagine the paratrooper.

[*The dim light goes completely out. A passage of blues piano is heard. It is an hour later. There is a spotlight on the writer as narrator, smoking at the foot of the cot, the sheet drawn about him like a toga.*]

WRITER: When I was alone in the room, the visitor having retreated beyond the plywood partition between his cubicle and mine, which was chalk white that turned ash-gray at night, not just he but everything visible was gone except for the lighter gray of the alcove with its window over Toulouse Street. An apparition came to me with the hypnotic effect of the painter's sandman special. It was in the form of an elderly female saint, of course. She materialized soundlessly. Her eyes fixed on me with a gentle questioning look which I came to remember as having belonged to my grandmother during her sieges of illness, when I used to go to her room and sit by her bed and want, so much, to say something or to put my hand over hers, but could do neither, knowing that if I did, I'd betray my feelings with tears that would trouble her more than her illness . . . Now it was she who stood next to my bed for a while. And as I drifted toward sleep, I wondered if she'd witnessed the encounter between the painter and me and what her attitude was toward such—perversions? Of longing?

[*The sound of stifled coughing is heard across the plywood partition.*]

26

Nothing about her gave me any sign. The weightless hands clasping each other so loosely, the cool and believing gray eyes in the faint pearly face were as immobile as statuary. I felt that she neither blamed nor approved the encounter. No. Wait. She . . . seemed to lift one hand very, very slightly before my eyes closed with sleep. An almost invisible gesture of . . . forgiveness? . . . through understanding? . . . before she dissolved into sleep . . .

Tye is in a seminarcotized state on the bed in Jane's room. Jane is in the hall burdened with paper sacks of groceries; the writer appears behind her.

JANE [*brightly*]: Good morning.

WRITER [*shyly*]: Oh, good morning.

JANE: Such a difficult operation, opening a purse with one hand.

WRITER: Let me hold the sacks for you.

JANE: Oh, thanks; now then, come in, put the sacks on one of those chairs. Over the weekend we run out of everything. Ice isn't delivered on Sundays, milk spoils. Everything of a perishable kind has got to be replaced. Oh, don't go out. Have you had a coffee?

WRITER [*looking at Tye*]: I was about to but . . .

JANE: Stay and have some with me. Sorry it's instant, can you stand instant coffee?

WRITER: I beg your pardon?

JANE: Don't mind him, when his eyes are half open it doesn't mean he is conscious.

TYE: Bullshit, you picked up a kid on the street?

JANE [*suppressing anger*]: This is the young man from across the hall—I'm Jane Sparks, my friend is Tye McCool, and you are—

WRITER [*pretending to observe a chess board to cover his embarrassment*]: What a beautiful chess board!

JANE: Oh, that, yes!

WRITER: Ivory and ebony? Figures?

JANE: The white squares are mother-of-pearl. Do you play chess?

WRITER: Used to. You play together, you and Mr.—McCool?

TYE: Aw, yeh, we play together but not chess. [*He rubs his crotch. Jane and the writer nervously study the chess board.*]

JANE: I play alone, a solitary game, to keep in practice in case I meet a partner.

WRITER: Look. Black is in check.

JANE: My imaginary opponent. I choose sides you see, although I play for both.

WRITER: I'd be happy to—I mean sometimes when you—

TYE [*touching the saucepan on the burner*]: OW!

JANE: I set it to boil before I went to the store.

[*Jane sets a cup and doughnuts on the table.*]

TYE: Hey, kid, why don't you take your cup across the hall to your own room?

JANE: Because I've just now—you heard me—invited him to have it here in this room with me.

TYE: I didn't invite him in, and I want you to git something straight: I live here. And if I live in a place I got equal rights in this place, and it just so happens I don't entertain no stranger to look at me undressed.

WRITER [*gulping down his coffee*]: Please. Uh, please, I think I'd rather go in my room because I, I've got some work to do there. I always work immediately after my coffee.

JANE: I will not have this young grifter who has established squatter's rights here telling me that I can't enjoy a little society in a place where—frankly I am frantic with loneliness!

[*The writer does not know what to do. Tye suddenly grins. He pulls out a chair for the writer at the table as if it were for a lady.*]

TYE: Have a seat kid, you like one lump or two? Where's the cat? Can I invite the goddam cat to breakfast?

JANE: Tye, you said you were pleased with the robe I gave you for your birthday, but you never wear it.

TYE: I don't dress for breakfast.

JANE: Putting on a silk robe isn't dressing.

[*She removes the robe from a hook and throws it about Tye's shoulders. Automatically he circles her hips with an arm.*]

TYE: Mmm. Good. Feels good.

JANE [*shyly disengaging herself from his embrace*]: It ought to. Shantung silk.

TYE: I didn't mean the robe, babe.

JANE: Tye, behave yourself. [*She turns to the writer.*] I've cherished the hope that by introducing Tye to certain little improvements in wearing apparel and language, I may gradually, despite his resistance—

TYE: Ain't that lovely? That classy langwidge she uses?

JANE: Inspire him to—seek out some higher level of employment. [*Ignoring Tye, she speaks.*] I heard that you are a writer?

WRITER: I, uh—write, but—

JANE: What form of writing? I mean fiction or poetry or . . .

TYE: Faggots, they all do something artistic, all of 'em.

JANE [*quickly*]: Do you know, I find myself drinking twice as much coffee here as I did in New York. For me the climate here is debilitating. Perhaps because of the dampness and the, and the—very low altitude, really there's no altitude at all, it's slightly under sea level. Have another cup with me?

[*The writer doesn't answer: Jane prepares two more cups of the instant coffee. Tye is staring steadily, challengingly at the writer, who appears to be hypnotized.*]

Of course, Manhattan hasn't much altitude either. But I grew up in the Adirondacks really. We lived on high ground, good elevation.

TYE: I met one of 'em once by accident on the street. You see, I was out of a job, and he came up to me on a corner in the Quarter an' invited me to his place for supper with him. I seen right off what he was an' what he wanted, but I didn't have the price of a poor boy sandwich so I accepted, I went. The place was all Japanese-like, everything very artistic. He said to me,

31

"Cross over that little bridge that crosses my little lake which I made myself and sit on the bench under my willow tree while I make supper for us and bathe an' change my clo'se. I won't be long." So I crossed over the bridge over the lake, and I stretched out under the weepin' willow tree: fell right asleep. I was woke up by what looked like a female but was him in drag. "Supper ready," he—she—said. Then this freak, put her hand on my—I said, "It's gonna cost you more than supper . . ."

JANE: Tye.

TYE: Huh, baby?

JANE: You will *not* continue that story.

TYE: It's a damn good story. What's your objection to it? I ain't got to the part that's really funny. [*He speaks to the writer, who is crossing out of the light.*] Don't you like the story?

[*The writer exits.*]

JANE: Why did you do that?

TYE: Do what?

JANE: You know what, and the boy knew what you meant by it. Why did you want to hurt him with the implication that he was in a class with a common, a predatory transvestite?

TYE: Look Jane . . . You say you was brought up on high ground, good elevation, but you come in here, you bring in here and expose me to a little queer, and . . .

JANE: Does everyone with civilized behavior, good manners, seem to be a queer to you?

32

TYE: . . . Was it good manners the way he looked at me, Babe?

JANE [*voice rising*]: Was it good manners for you to stand in front of him rubbing your—groin the way you did?

TYE: I wanted you to notice his reaction.

JANE: He was just embarrassed.

TYE: You got a lot to learn about life in the Quarter.

JANE: I think that he's a serious person that I can talk to, and I need some one to talk to!

[*Pause*]

TYE: You can't talk to *me* huh?

JANE: With you working all night at a Bourbon Street strip-joint, and sleeping nearly all day? Involving yourself with all the underworld elements of this corrupt city . . .

TYE: 'Sthat all I do? Just that? I never pleasure you, Babe?

[*Fade in piano blues. She draws a breath and moves as if half asleep behind Tye's chair.*]

JANE: Yes, you—pleasure me, Tye.

TYE: I try to do my best to, Babe. Sometimes I wonder why a girl—

JANE: Not a girl, Tye. A woman.

TYE: —How did—why did—you get yourself mixed up with me?

JANE: A sudden change of circumstances removed me from—
how shall I put it so you'd understand?

TYE: Just—say.

JANE: What I'd thought was myself. So I quit my former
connections, I came down here to—[*She stops short.*] Well, to
make an adjustment to—[*Pause.*] We met by chance on Royal
Street when a deluge of rain backed me into a doorway. Didn't
know you were behind me until you put your hand on my hip
and I turned to say, "Stop that!" but didn't because you were
something I'd never encountered before—faintly innocent—boy's
eyes. Smiling. Said to myself, "Why not, with nothing to lose!"
Of course you pleasure me, Tye!—I'd been alone so long . . .

[*She touches his throat with trembling fingers. He leans
sensually back against her. She runs her hand down his chest.*]

Silk on silk is—lovely . . . regardless of the danger.

[*As the light on this area dims, typing begins offstage. The
dim-out is completed.*]

SCENE FOUR

A lighted area represents Mrs. Wire's kitchen, in which she is preparing a big pot of gumbo despite the hour, which is midnight. She could be mistaken for a witch from Macbeth *in vaguely modern but not new costume.*

The writer's footsteps catch her attention. He appears at the edge of the light in all that remains of his wardrobe: riding boots and britches, a faded red flannel shirt.

MRS. WIRE: Who, who?—Aw, you, dressed up like a jockey in a donkey race!

WRITER: —My, uh, clothes are at the cleaners.

MRS. WIRE: Do they clean clothes at the pawnshop, yeah, I reckon they do clean clothes not redeemed. Oh. Don't go upstairs. Your room is forfeited, too.

WRITER: . . . You mean I'm . . . ?

MRS. WIRE: A loser, boy. Possibly you could git a cot at the Salvation Army.

WRITER [*averting his eyes*]: May I sit down a moment?

MRS. WIRE: Why, for what?

WRITER: Eviction presents . . . a problem.

MRS. WIRE: I thought you was gittin' on the WPA Writers' Project? That's what you tole me when I inquired about your prospects for employment, you said, "Oh, I've applied for work on the WPA for writers."

WRITER: I couldn't prove that my father was destitute, and the

fact he contributes nothing to my support seemed—immaterial
to them.

MRS. WIRE: Why're you shifty-eyed? I never seen a more
shifty-eyed boy.

WRITER: I, uh, have had a little eye trouble, lately.

MRS. WIRE: You're gettin' a cataract on your left eye, boy,
face it!—Cataracts don't usually hit at your age.

WRITER: I've noticed a lot of things have hit me—prema-
turely . . .

MRS. WIRE [*stirring gumbo*]: Hungry? I bet. I eat at irregular
hours. I suddenly got a notion to cook up a gumbo, and when I
do, the smell of it is an attraction, draws company in the
kitchen. Oh ho—footsteps fast. Here comes the ladies.

WRITER: Mrs. Wire, those old ladies are starving, dying of
malnutrition.

[*Miss Carrie and Mary Maude appear at the edge of the
lighted area with queer, high-pitched laughter or some bizarre
relation to laughter.*]

MRS. WIRE: Set back down there, boy. [*Pause.*] Why, Mizz
Wayne an' Miss Carrie, you girls still up at this hour!

MISS CARRIE: We heard you moving about and wondered if
we could . . .

MARY MAUDE: Be of some assistance.

MRS. WIRE: Shoot, Mrs. Wayne, do you imagine that rusty ole
saucepan of yours is invisible to me? Why, I know when I put

this gumbo on the stove and lit the fire, it would smoke you ladies out of your locked room. What do you all do in that locked room so much?

MARY MAUDE: We keep ourselves occupied.

MISS CARRIE: We are compiling a cookbook which we hope to have published. A Creole cookbook, recipes we remember from our childhood.

MRS. WIRE: A recipe is a poor substitute for food.

MARY MAUDE [*with a slight breathless pause*]: We ought to go out more regularly for meals but our . . . our light bulbs have burned out, so we can't distinguish night from day anymore. Only shadows come in.

MISS CARRIE: Sshh! [*Pause.*] Y'know, I turned down an invitation to dinner this evening at my cousin Mathilde Devereau Pathet's in the Garden District.

MRS. WIRE: Objected to the menu?

MISS CARRIE: No, but you know, very rich people are so inconsiderate sometimes. With four limousines and drivers at their constant disposal, they wouldn't send one to fetch me.

MRS. WIRE: Four? Limousines? Four drivers?

[*A delicate, evanescent music steals in as the scene acquires a touch of the bizarre. At moments the players seem bewildered as if caught in a dream.*]

MISS CARRIE: Oh, yes, four, four . . . spanking new Cadillacs with uniformed chauffeurs!

37

MRS. WIRE: Now, that's very impressive.

MISS CARRIE: They call Mr. Pathet the "Southern Planter."

MRS. WIRE: Has a plantation, in the Garden District?

MISS CARRIE [*gasping*]: Oh, no, no, no, no. He's a mortician, most prominent mortician, buries all the best families in the parish.

MRS. WIRE: And poor relations, too? I hope.

MARY MAUDE: Miss Carrie goes into a family vault when she goes.

MRS. WIRE: When?

MARY MAUDE: Yes, above ground, has a vault reserved in . . .

MISS CARRIE: Let's not speak of that! . . . now.

MRS. WIRE: Why not speak of that? You got to consider the advantage of this connection. Because of the expenses of "The Inevitable" someday soon, 'specially with your asthma? No light? And bad nutrition?

MISS CARRIE: The dampness of the old walls in the Quarter—you know how they hold damp. This city is actually eight feet below sea level. Niggers are buried under the ground, and their caskets fill immediately with water.

MRS. WIRE: But I reckon your family vault is above this nigger water level?

MISS CARRIE: Oh, yes, above water level, in fact, I'll be on top of my great-great-uncle, Jean Pierre Devereau, the third.

[*The writer laughs a bit, involuntarily. The ladies glare at him.*]

Mrs. Wire, who is this . . . transient? Young man?

MARY MAUDE: We did understand that this was a guesthouse, not a . . . refuge for delinquents.

MISS CARRIE [*turning her back on the writer*]: They do set an exquisite table at the Pathets, with excellent food, but it's not appetizing, you know, to be conducted on a tour of inspection of the business display room, you know, the latest model of caskets on display, and that's what René Pathet does, invariably escorts me, proud as a peacock, through the coffin display rooms before . . . we sit down to dinner. And all through dinner, he discusses his latest clients and . . . those expected shortly.

MRS. WIRE: Maybe he wants you to pick out your casket cause he's noticed your asthma from damp walls in the Quarter.

MISS CARRIE: I do, of course, understand that business is business with him, a night and day occupation.

MRS. WIRE: You know, I always spit in a pot of gumbo to give it special flavor, like a bootblack spits on a shoe. [*She pretends to spit in the pot. The crones try to laugh.*] Now help yourself, fill your saucepan full, and I'll loan you a couple of spoons, but let it cool a while, don't blister your gums . . . [*She hands them spoons.*] . . . and Mrs. Wayne, I'll be watching the mailbox for Buster's army paycheck.

MARY MAUDE: That boy has never let me down, he's the most devoted son a mother could hope for.

MRS. WIRE: Yais, if she had no hope.

MARY MAUDE: I got a postcard from him . . .

MRS. WIRE: A postcard can't be cashed.

MARY MAUDE [*diverting Mrs. Wire's attention, she hopes, as Miss Carrie ladles out gumbo*]: Of course, I wasn't prepared for the circumstance that struck me when I discovered that Mr. Wayne had not kept up his insurance payments, *that* I was not prepared for, that it was *lapsed.*

MRS. WIRE [*amused*]: I bet you wasn't prepared for a little surprise like that.

MARY MAUDE: No, not for that nor for the discovery that secretly for years he'd been providing cash and real estate to that little redheaded doxy he'd kept in Bay St. Louie.

MISS CARRIE: Owwwww!

[*Mrs. Wire whirls about, and Miss Carrie is forced to swallow the scalding mouthful.*]

MRS. WIRE: I bet that mouthful scorched your throat, Miss Carrie. Didn't I tell you to wait?

MARY MAUDE: Carrie, give me that saucepan before you spill it, your hand's so shaky. Thank you, Mrs. Wire. Carrie, thank Mrs. Wire for her being so concerned always about our— circumstances here. Now let's go and see what can be done for that throat. [*They move toward the stairs but do not exit.*]

MRS. WIRE: Cut it, if all else fails.

[*Something crashes on the stairs. All turn that way. Tye appears dimly, bearing two heavy cartons; he speaks to the writer, who is nearest to him.*]

40

TYE: Hey, you, boy?

WRITER: —Me?

TYE: Yeh, yeh, you, I dropped one of these packages on th' steps, so goddam dark I dropped it. And I'd appreciate it if you'd pick it up fo' me an' help me git it upstairs.

WRITER: I'll be—glad to try to . . .

[*Tye focuses dimly on Miss Carrie. He blinks several times in disbelief.*]

TYE: Am I . . . in the right place?

MRS. WIRE [*shouting*]: Not in your present condition. Go on back out. Sleep it off in the gutter.

MISS CARRIE [*to Mrs. Wire*]: Tragic for such a nice-looking young man to return to his wife in that condition at night.

MRS. WIRE: Practically every night.

[*Miss Carrie and Mary Maude exit.*

[*Tye has almost miraculously managed to collect his dropped packages, and he staggers to stage right where the lower steps to the attic are dimly seen. The writer follows.*]

TYE [*stumbling back against the writer*]: Can you make it? Can you make it, kid?

[*They slowly mount the steps. The lighted kitchen is dimmed out. There is a brief pause. A soft light is cast on the attic hall.*]

TYE: Now, kid, can you locate my room key in my pocket?

41

WRITER: Which, uh—pocket?

TYE: Pan's pocket.

WRITER: Left pocket or—

TYE: —Head—spinnin'—money in hip pocket, key in—right—lef' side. Shit—key befo' I—fall . . .

[*The writer's hand starts to enter a pocket when Tye collapses, spilling the boxes on the floor and sprawling across them.*]

WRITER: You're right outside my cubbyhole. I suggest you rest in there before you—wake up your wife . . .

TYE: M'ole lady, she chews my ass off if I come home this ways . . . [*He struggles heroically to near standing position as the writer guides him into his cubicle.*] . . . This—bed?

[*There is a soft, ghostly laugh from the adjoining cubicle. A match strikes briefly.*]

WRITER: Swing your legs the other way, that way's the pillow—would you, uh, like your wet shoes off?

TYE: Shoes? Yes, but nothin' else. Once I—passed out on—Bourbon Street—late night—in a dark doorway—woke up—this guy, was takin' liberties with me and I don't go for that stuff—

WRITER: I don't take advantages of that kind, I am—going back downstairs, if you're comfortable now . . .

TYE: I said to this guy, "Okay, if you wanto blow me, you can pay me one hunnerd dollars—before, not after."

[*Tye's voice dies out. Nightingale becomes visible, rising stealthily in his cubicle and slipping on a robe, as Tye begins to snore.*

[*The attic lights dim out. The lights on the kitchen come up as the writer re-enters.*]

MRS. WIRE: Got that bum to bed? Set down, son. Ha! Notice I called you, son. Where do you go nights?

WRITER: Oh, I walk, I take long solitary walks. Sometimes I . . . I . . .

MRS. WIRE: Sometimes you what? You can say it's none of my business, but I, well, I have a sort of a, well you could say I have a sort of a—maternal—concern. You see, I do have a son that I never see no more, but I worry about him so I reckon it's natural for me to worry about you a little. And get things straight in my head about you—you've changed since you've been in this house. You know that?

WRITER: Yes, I know that.

MRS. WIRE: This I'll tell you, when you first come to my door, I swear I seen and I recognized a young gentleman in you—shy. Shaky, but . . .

WRITER: Panicky! Yes! Gentleman? My folks say so. I wonder.

[*The light narrows and focuses on the writer alone; the speech becomes an interior reflection.*]

I've noticed I do have some troublesome little scruples in my nature that may cause difficulties in my . . . [*He rises and rests his foot on the chair.*] . . . negotiated—truce with—life. Oh— there's a price for things, that's something I've learned in the

43

Vieux Carré. For everything that you purchase in this market-place you pay out of *here!* [*He thumps his chest.*] And the cash which is the stuff you use in your work can be overdrawn, depleted, like a reservoir going dry in a long season of drought . . .

[*The scene is resumed on a realistic level with a change in the lighting.*]

MRS. WIRE [*passing a bowl of gumbo to the writer*]: Here, son, have some gumbo. Let it cool a while. I just pretended to spit in it, you know.

WRITER: I know.

MRS. WIRE: I make the best gumbo, I do the best Creole cookin' in Louisiana. It's God's truth, and now I'll tell you what I'm plannin' to do while your gumbo's coolin'. I'll tell you because it involves a way you could pay your room and board here.

WRITER: Oh?

MRS. WIRE: Uh huh, I'm plannin' to open a lunchroom.

WRITER: On the premises? Here?

MRS. WIRE: On the premises, in my bedroom, which I'm gonna convert into a small dinin' room. So I'm gonna git printed up some bus'ness cards. At twelve noon ev'ry day except Sundays you can hit the streets with these little bus'ness cards announcin' that lunch is bein' served for twenty-five cents, a cheaper lunch than you could git in a greasy spoon on Chartres . . . and no better cooking in the Garden District or the Vieux Carré.

WRITER: Meals for a quarter in the Quarter.

MRS. WIRE: Hey! That's the slogan! I'll print it on those cards that you'll pass out.

WRITER [*dreamily*]: Wonderful gumbo.

MRS. WIRE: Why this "Meals for a quarter in the Quarter" is going to put me back in the black, yeah! Boy! . . . [*She throws him the key to his attic rooms. The lights dim out briefly.*]

TYE'S VOICE: Hey! Whatcha doin'? Git yuh fuckin' hands off me!

[*The writer appears dimly in the attic hall outside his room. He stops.*]

NIGHTINGALE'S VOICE: I thought that I was visiting a friend.

TYE'S VOICE: 'Sthat how you visit a friend, unzippin' his pants an' pullin' out his dick?

NIGHTINGALE'S VOICE: I assure you it was a mistake of—identity . . .

TYE [*becoming visible on the side of the bed in the writer's cubicle*]: This ain't my room. Where is my ole lady? Hey, *hey, Jane!*

WRITER: You collapsed in the hall outside your door so I helped you in here.

TYE: Both of you git this straight. No goddam faggot messes with me, never! For less'n a hundred dollars!

[*Jane becomes visible in the hall before this line.*]

45

A hunnerd dollars, yes, maybe, but not a dime less.

NIGHTINGALE [*emerging from the cubicle in his robe*]: I am afraid that you have priced yourself out of the market.

JANE: Tye, come out of there.

TYE: I been interfered with 'cause you'd locked me out.

WRITER: Miss, uh, Sparks, I didn't touch your friend except to, to . . . offer him my bed till you let him in.

JANE: Tye, stand up—if you can stand! Stand. Walk.

[*Tye stumbles against her, and she cries out as she is pushed against the wall.*]

TYE'S VOICE: Locked out, bolted outa my room, to be—molested.

JANE: I heard you name a price, with you everything has a price. Thanks, good night.

[*During this exchange Nightingale in his purple robe has leaned, smoking with a somewhat sardonic look, against the partition between the two cubicles. The writer reappears.*]

NIGHTINGALE: Back so quick?—*Tant pis* . . .

WRITER: I think if I were you, I'd go in your own room and get to bed.

[*The writer enters his cubicle. Nightingale's face slowly turns to a mask of sorrow past expression. There is music. Nightingale puts out his cigarette and enters his cubicle.*

46

[Jane undresses Tye. The writer undresses. Nightingale sits on his cot. Tye and Jane begin to make love. Downstairs, Nursie mops the floor, singing to herself. The writer moves slowly to his bed and places his hand on the warm sheets that Tye has left. The light dims.

[There is a passage of time.]

The attic rooms are dimly lit. Nightingale is adjusting a necker-chief about his wasted throat. He enters the writer's cubicle without knocking.

NIGHTINGALE: May I intrude once more? It's embarrassing—this incident. Not of any importance, nothing worth a second thought. [*He coughs.*] Oh Christ. You know my mattress is full of bedbugs. Last night I smashed one at least the size of my thumbnail, it left a big blood spot on the pillow. [*He coughs and gasps for breath.*] I showed it to the colored woman that the witch calls Nursie, and Nursie told her about it, and she came charging up here and demanded that I exhibit the bug, which I naturally . . . [*A note of uncertainty and fear enters his voice.*]

WRITER: . . . removed from the pillow.

NIGHTINGALE: Who in hell wouldn't remove the remains of a squashed bedbug from his pillow? Nobody I'd want social or any acquaintance with . . . she even . . . intimated that I coughed up the blood, as if I had . . . [*coughs*] consumption.

WRITER [*stripped to his shorts and about to go to bed*]: I think with that persistent cough of yours you should get more rest.

NIGHTINGALE: Restlessness. Insomnia. I can't imagine a worse affliction, and I've suffered from it nearly all my life. I consulted a doctor about it once, and he said, "You don't sleep because it reminds you of death." A ludicrous assumption—the only true regret I'd have over leaving this world is that I'd leave so much of my serious work unfinished.

WRITER [*holding the bedsheet up to his chin*]: Do show me your serious work.

NIGHTINGALE: I know why you're taking this tone.

WRITER: I am not taking any tone.

NIGHTINGALE: Oh yes you are, you're very annoyed with me because my restlessness, my loneliness, made me so indiscreet as to—offer my attentions to that stupid but—physically appealing young man you'd put on that cot with the idea of reserving him for yourself. And so I do think your tone is a bit hypocritical, don't you?

WRITER: All right, I do admit I find him attractive, too, but I did *not* make a pass at him.

NIGHTINGALE: I heard him warn you.

WRITER: I simply removed his wet shoes.

NIGHTINGALE: Little man, you are sensual, but I, I—am rapacious.

WRITER: And I am tired.

NIGHTINGALE: Too tired to return my visits? Not very appreciative of you, but lack of appreciation is something I've come to expect and almost to accept as if God—the alleged—had stamped on me a sign at birth—"This man will offer himself and not be accepted, not by anyone ever!"

WRITER: Please don't light that candle.

NIGHTINGALE: I shall, the candle is lit.

WRITER: I do wish that you'd return to your side of the wall—well, now I am taking a tone, but it's . . . justified. Now do

49

please get out, get out, I mean it, when I blow out the candle I want to be alone.

NIGHTINGALE: You know, you're going to grow into a selfish, callous man. Returning no visits, reciprocating no . . . caring.

WRITER: . . . Why do you predict that?

NIGHTINGALE: That little opacity on your left eye pupil could mean a like thing happening to your heart. [*He sits on the cot.*]

WRITER: You have to protect your heart.

NIGHTINGALE: With a shell of calcium? Would that improve your work?

WRITER: You talk like you have a fever, I . . .

NIGHTINGALE: I have a fever you'd be lucky to catch, a fever to hold and be held! [*He throws off his tattered silk robe.*] Hold me! Please, please hold me.

WRITER: I'm afraid I'm tired, I need to sleep and . . . I don't want to catch your cold.

[*Slowly with dignity, Nightingale rises from the cot and puts his silk robe on.*]

NIGHTINGALE: And I don't want to catch yours, which is a cold in the heart, that's a hell of a lot more fatal to a boy with literary pretensions.

[*This releases in the writer a cold rage which he has never felt before. He springs up and glares at Nightingale, who is coughing.*]

50

WRITER [*in a voice quick and hard as a knife*]: I think there has been some deterioration in your condition and you ought to face it! A man has got to face everything sometime and call it by its true name, not to try to escape it by—cowardly!—evasion— go have your lungs x-rayed and don't receive the doctor's bill when it's sent! But go there quick, have the disease stated clearly! Don't, don't call it a cold anymore or a touch of the flu!

NIGHTINGALE [*turning with a gasp*]: You've gone mad, you've gone out of your mind here, you little one-eyed bitch! [*He coughs again and staggers out of the light.*]

MRS. WIRE'S VOICE: I heard you from the kitchen, boy! Was he molesting you in here? I heard him. Was he molesting you in here? Speak up! [*Her tone loses its note of concern as she shouts to Nightingale.*] You watch out, I'll get the goods on you yet!

NIGHTINGALE'S VOICE: The persecution continues.

||||||||||||||||||||||||||||||||||||||||||||||||||||||||||||||||||||||||||||||||||||||||||||||||||||||||||||||||

Daylight appears in the alcove window—daylight tinged with rain. The room of Jane and Tye is lighted. Tye is sprawled, apparently sleeping, in shorts on the studio bed. Jane has just completed a fashion design. She stares at it with disgust, then crumples it and throws it to the floor with a sob of frustration.

||||||||||||||||||||||||||||||||||||||||||||||||||||||||||||||||||||||||||||||||||||||||||||||||||||||||||||||||

JANE: Yes? Who's there?

WRITER: Uh, me, from across the hall, I brought in a letter for you—it was getting rained on.

JANE: Oh, one moment, please. [*She throws a robe over her panties and bra and opens the door.*] A letter for me?

WRITER: The mail gets wet when it rains since the lid's come off the mailbox.

[*His look irresistibly takes in the figure of Tye. Jane tears the letter open and gasps softly. She looks slowly up, with a stunned expression, at the young writer.*]

JANE: Would you care for some coffee?

WRITER: Thanks, no, I just take it in the morning.

JANE: Then please have a drink with me. I need a drink. Please, please come in. [*Jane is speaking hysterically but abruptly controls it.*] Excuse me—would you pour the drinks—I can't. I . . .

WRITER [*crossing to the cabinet*]: Will you have . . .

JANE: Bourbon. Three fingers.

WRITER: With?

JANE: Nothing, nothing.

[*The writer glances again at Tye as he pours the bourbon.*]

Nothing . . . [*The writer crosses to her with the drink.*] Nothing. And you?

WRITER: Nothing, thanks. I have to retype the manuscripts soaked in the rain.

JANE: *Manuscripts*, you said? Oh, yes, you're a writer. I knew, it just slipped my mind. The manuscripts were returned? Does that mean rejection? —Rejection is always so painful.

WRITER [*with shy pride*]: This time instead of a printed slip there was this personal signed note . . .

JANE: Encouraging—that. Oh, my glass is weeping—an Italian expression. Would you play barman again? Please? [*She doesn't know where to put the letter, which he keeps glancing at.*]

WRITER: Yes, I am encouraged. He says, "This one doesn't quite make it but try us again." *Story* magazine—they print William Saroyan, you know!

JANE: It takes a good while to get established in a creative field.

WRITER: And meanwhile you've got to survive.

JANE: I was lucky, but the luck didn't hold. [*She is taking little sips of the straight bourbon.*]

WRITER: You're—upset by that—letter? I noticed it came from— isn't Ochsner's à clinic?

53

JANE: Yes, actually. I am, I was. It concerns a relative rather—critically ill there.

WRITER: Someone close to you?

JANE: Yes. Quite close, although lately I hardly recognize the lady at all anymore . . .

[*Tye stirs on the bed; the writer irresistibly glances at him.*]

Pull the sheet over him. I think he unconsciously displays himself like that as if posing for a painter of sensual inclinations. Wasted on me. I just illustrate fashions for ladies.

TYE [*stirring*]: Beret? Beret?

[*The writer starts off, pausing at the edge of the light.*]

WRITER: Jane, what was the letter, wasn't it about you?

JANE: Let's just say it was a sort of a personal, signed rejection slip, too.

[*The writer exits with a backward glance.*]

TYE: Where's Beret, where's the goddam cat?

[*Jane is fiercely tearing the letter to bits. The lights dim out.*]

SCENE SEVEN

A dim light comes up on the writer, stage front, as narrator.

IIIIIIIIIIIIIIIIIIIIIIIIIIIIIIIIIIIIIIIIIIIIIIIIIIIIIIIIIIIIIIIIIIIIIIIIIIIIIIIIIIIIIIIIIIIIIIIIIIIIIIIIIIIIII

WRITER: The basement of the building had been leased by Mrs. Wire to a fashionable youngish photographer, one T. Hamilton Biggs, a very effete man he was, who had somehow acquired a perfect Oxford accent in Baton Rouge, Louisiana. He made a good living in New Orleans out of artfully lighted photos of debutantes and society matrons in the Garden District, but for his personal amusement—he also photographed, more realistically, some of the many young drifters to be found along the streets of the Vieux Carré.

[*The lights go up on the kitchen. Mrs. Wire is seen at the stove, which bears steaming pots of water.*]

MRS. WIRE [*to the writer*]: Aw, it's you sneakin' in at two A.M. like a thief.

WRITER: Yes, uh, good night.

MRS. WIRE: Hold on, don't go up yet. He's at it again down there, he's throwin' one of his orgies, and this'll be the last one he throws down there. By God an' by Jesus, the society folk in this city may tolerate vice but not me. Take one of them pots off the stove.

WRITER: You're, uh . . . cooking at this hour?

MRS. WIRE: Not cooking . . . I'm boiling water! I take this pot and you take the other one, we'll pour this water through the hole in this kitchen floor, which is directly over that studio of his!

WRITER: Mrs. Wire, I can't be involved in . . .

55

MRS. WIRE: Boy, you're employed by me, you're fed and housed here, and you do like I tell you or you'll go on the street. [*She lifts a great kettle off the stove.*] Take that pot off the stove! [*She empties the steaming water on the floor. Almost instant screams are heard below.*] Hahh, down there, what's the disturbance over?!

WRITER: Mrs. Wire, that man has taken out a peace warrant against you, you know that.

MRS. WIRE: Git out of my way, you shifty-eyed little— [*With demonical energy she seizes the other pot and empties it onto the floor, and the screams continue. She looks and runs to the proscenium as if peering out a window.*] Two of 'em run out naked. Got two of you, I'm not done with you yet! . . . you perverts!

WRITER: Mrs. Wire, he'll call the police.

MRS. WIRE: Let him, just let him, my nephew is a lieutenant on the police force! But these Quarter police, why anybody can buy 'em, and that Biggs, he's got big money. Best we be quiet, sit tight. Act real casual-like. If they git in that door, you seen a, you seen a—

WRITER: What?

MRS. WIRE: A drunk spillin' water in here.

WRITER: . . . that much water?

MRS. WIRE: *Hush up!* One contradictory word out of you and I'll brain you with this saucepan here.

[*Nightingale enters in his robe.*]

NIGHTINGALE: May I inquire what this bedlam is about? [*He pants for breath.*] I had just finally managed to . . . [*He gasps.*] This hellish disturbance . . .

MRS. WIRE: May you inquire, yeah, you may inquire. Look. Here's the story! You're in a doped-up condition. Drunk and doped-up you staggered against the stove and accidentally knocked a kettle of boiling water off it. Now that's the story you'll tell in payment of back rent and your habits! . . . disgracing my house!

NIGHTINGALE [*to writer*]: *What* is she talking about?

MRS. WIRE: And *you . . . one eye!* [*She turns to the writer.*] You say you witnessed it, you back up the story, you heah?

WRITER [*grinning*]: Mrs. Wire, the story wouldn't . . . hold water.

MRS. WIRE: I said accidental. In his condition who'd doubt it?

NIGHTINGALE: Hoo, hoo, hoo!

MRS. WIRE: That night court buzzard on the bench, he'd throw the book at me for no reason but the fight that I've put up against the corruption and evil that this Quarter is built on! All I'm asking is . . .

[*Abruptly Miss Carrie and Mary Maude in outrageous negligees burst into the kitchen. At the sight of them, Mrs. Wire starts to scream wordlessly as a peacock at a pitch that stuns the writer but not Nightingale and the crones. Just as abruptly she falls silent and flops into a chair.*]

MISS CARRIE: Oh, Mrs. Wire!

MARY MAUDE: We thought the house had caught fire!

NIGHTINGALE [*loftily*]: . . . What a remarkable . . . *tableau vivant* . . . The paddy wagon's approaching. Means night court, you know.

WRITER: . . . I think I'll . . . go to bed now . . .

MRS. WIRE: Like shoot you will!

[*Jane appears, stage right, in a robe. She speaks to the writer, who is nearest to her.*]

JANE: Can you tell me what is going on down here?

WRITER: Miss Sparks, why don't you stay in your room right now?

JANE: Why?

WRITER: There's been a terrible incident down here, I think the police are coming.

[*Mary Maude screams, wringing her hands.*]

MARY MAUDE: Police!

MISS CARRIE: Oh, Mary Maude, this is not time for hysterics. You're not involved, nor am I! We simply came in to see what the disturbance was about.

JANE [*to the writer*]: Was Tye here? Was Tye involved in this . . .

WRITER [*in a low voice to Jane*]: Nobody was involved but Mrs. Wire. She poured boiling water through a hole in the floor.

MRS. WIRE [*like a field marshal*]: Everybody in here stay here and sit tight till the facts are reported.

[*Nursie enters with black majesty. She is humming a church hymn softly, "He walks with me and he talks with me." She remains at the edge of the action, calm as if unaware.*]

I meant ev'ry goddam one of you except Nursie. Nursie! Don't stand there singin' gospel, barefoot, in that old dirty nightgown!

WRITER [*to Jane*]: She wants us to support a totally false story.

MRS. WIRE: I tell you—the Vieux Carré is the new Babylon destroyed by evil in Scriptures!!

JANE: It's like a dream . . .

NIGHTINGALE: The photographer downstairs belongs to the Chateau family, one of the finest and most important families in the Garden District.

MRS. WIRE: Oh, do you write the social register now?

NIGHTINGALE: I know he is New Orleans's most prominent society photographer!

MRS. WIRE: I know he's the city's most notorious *per*vert and is occupying space in my building!

MISS CARRIE: Mary Maude and I can't afford the notoriety of a thing like this.

[*Mary Maude cries out and leans against the table.*]

MARY MAUDE: Mrs. Wire, Miss Carrie and I have—positions to maintain!

59

JANE: Mrs. Wire, surely there's no need for these ladies to be involved in this.

MRS. WIRE: Deadbeats, all, all! Will stay right here and—

JANE: Do what?

MRS. WIRE: —testify to what happened!

NIGHTINGALE: She wishes you all to corroborate her lie! That I, that I! Oh, yes, I'm appointed to assume responsibility for—

PHOTOGRAPHER [*off stage*]: Right up there! Burns like this could disfigure me for life!

[*Mrs. Wire rushes to slam and bolt the door.*]

MISS CARRIE [*to Mary Maude*]: Honey? Can you move now?

MRS. WIRE: No, she cain't, she stays—which applies to you all!

PHOTOGRAPHER: The fact that she is insane and allowed to remain at large . . . doesn't excuse it.

[*A patrolman bangs at the door.*]

MRS. WIRE: Shh! Nobody make a sound!

PHOTOGRAPHER: Not only she but her tenants; why, the place is a psycho ward.

[*More banging is heard.*]

MRS. WIRE: What's this banging about?

PATROLMAN: Open this door.

60

ıımıımıımıımıımıımıımıımıımıımıımıımıımıımıımıımıımıımıımıımıımıımıımıımıımıımıımıımıımıımıım

PHOTOGRAPHER: One of my guests was the nephew of the District Attorney!

PATROLMAN: Open or I'll force it.

PHOTOGRAPHER: Break it in! Kick it open!

MRS. WIRE [*galvanized*]: You ain't comin' in here, you got no warrant to enter, you filthy—morphodite, you!

WRITER: Mrs. Wire, you said not to make a sound.

MRS. WIRE: Make no sound when they're breakin' in my house, you one-eyed Jack? [*The banging continues.*] What's the meaning of this, wakin' me up at two A.M. in the mawnin'?

PHOTOGRAPHER: Scalded! Five guests, including two art models!

MRS. WIRE [*overlapping*]: You broken the terms of your lease, and it's now broke. I rented you that downstair space for legitimate business, you turned it into a—continual awgy!

PATROLMAN: Open that door, ma'am, people have been seriously injured.

MRS. WIRE: That's no concern of mine! I open no door till I phone my nephew, a lieutenant on the police force, Jim Flynn, who knows the situation I've put up with here, and then we'll see who calls the law on who!

WRITER: I hear more police sirens comin'.

[*The pounding and shouting continue. A patrolman forces entry, followed by another. All during the bit just preceding, Miss Carie and Mary Maude have clung together, their terri-*

61

fied whispers maintaining a low-pitched threnody to the shouting and banging. Now as the two patrolmen enter, their hysteria erupts in shrill screams. The screams are so intense that the patrolmen's attention is directed upon them.]

PATROLMAN 1: Christ! Is this a fuckin' madhouse?

[*Still clinging together, the emaciated crones sink to their knees as if at the feet of an implacable deity.*]

MRS. WIRE [*inspired*]: Officers, remove these demented, old horrors. Why, you know what they done? Poured water on the floor of my kitchen, boiling water!

NIGHTINGALE: She's lying. These unfortunate old ladies just came in, they thought the house was on fire.

PHOTOGRAPHER: This woman is the notorious Mrs. Wire, and it was she who screamed out the window. Why, these old women should be hospitalized, naturally, but it's her, her! [*He points at Mrs. Wire from the door.*] that poured the scalding water into my studio, and screamed with delight when my art models and guests ran naked into the street!

MRS. WIRE: There, now, AWGY CONFESSED!!

PATROLMAN 2: All out to the wagon!

[*The scene is dimmed out fast. A spot comes up on the writer in the witness box at night court.*]

OLD JUDGE'S VOICE: Let's not have no more beatin' aroun' the bush in this court, young fellow. The question is plain. You're under oath to give an honest answer. Now for the last time, at risk of being held in contempt of court, "Did you or did you not see the proprietor of the rooming house . . ."

MRS. WIRE'S VOICE [*shrilly*]: Restaurant and roomin' house respectfully run!

[*The judge pounds his gavel.*]

OLD JUDGE'S VOICE: Defendant will keep silent during the witness' testimony. To repeat the question: "Did you or did you not see this lady here pour boiling water through the floor of her kitchen down into the studio of Mr. T. Hamilton Biggs?"

WRITER [*swallows, then in a low voice*]: I, uh . . . think it's unlikely . . . a lady would do such a thing.

OLD JUDGE'S VOICE: Speak up so I can heah you! What's that you said?

WRITER: . . . I said I thought it very unlikely a lady would do such a thing.

[*Laughter is heard in the night court. The judge gavels, then pronounces the verdict.*]

OLD JUDGE'S VOICE: This court finds the defendant, Mrs. Hortense Wire, guilty as charged and imposes a fine of fifty dollars plus damages and releases her on probation in the custody of her nephew, Police Lieutenant James Flynn of New Orleans Parish, for a period of . . .

[*His voice fades out as does the scene. A spotlight comes up on Mrs. Wire in a flannel robe, drinking at the kitchen table. The writer appears hesitantly at the edge of the kitchen light.*]

MRS. WIRE [*without turning*]: I know you're standing there, but I don't wanta see you. It sure does surprise me that you'd dare to enter this house again after double-crossing me in court tonight.

WRITER: —I—just came back to pick up my things.

MRS. WIRE: You ain't gonna remove nothing from this place till you paid off what you owe me.

WRITER: You know I'm—destitute.

MRS. WIRE: You get tips from the customers.

WRITER: Nickels and dimes. [*Pause. The sound of rain is heard.*] —Mrs. Wire? [*She turns slowly to look at him.*] Do you think I really intended to lose you that case? Other witnesses had testified I was in the kitchen when you poured those kettles of water through the floor. And the judge knew I could see with at least one eye. I was on the witness stand under oath, couldn't perjure myself. I did try not to answer directly. I *didn't* answer directly. All I said was—

MRS. WIRE: You said what lost me the case, goddam it! Did you expect that old buzzard on the bench to mistake me for a lady, my hair in curlers, me wearin' the late, long ago Mr. Wire's old ragged bathrobe. Shoot! All of you witnesses betrayed me in night court because you live off me an' can't forgive me for it.

WRITER: —I guess you want me to go . . .

MRS. WIRE: To where would you go? How far could you get on your nickels and dimes? You're shiverin' like a wet dog. Set down. Have a drink with me befo' you go up to bed.

WRITER: You mean I can stay? [*She nods slightly. He sits down at the kitchen table; she pours him a drink.*] I don't think I ever saw you drink before, Mrs. Wire.

MRS. WIRE: I only touch this bottle, which also belonged to the late Mr. Wire before he descended to hell between two crooked lawyers, I touch it only when forced to by such a shocking experience as I had tonight, the discovery that I was completely alone in the world, a solitary ole woman cared for by no one. You know, I heard some doctor say on the radio that people die of loneliness, specially at my age. They do. Die of it, it kills 'em. Oh, that's not the cause that's put on the death warrant, but that's the *true* cause. I tell you, there's so much loneliness in this house that you can hear it. Set still and you can hear it: a sort of awful—soft—groaning in all the walls.

WRITER: All I hear is rain on the roof.

MRS. WIRE: You're still too young to hear it, but I hear it and I feel it, too, like a—ache in ev'ry bone of my body. It makes me want to scream, but I got to keep still. A landlady ain't permitted to scream. It would disturb the tenants. But some time I will, I'll scream, I'll scream loud enough to bring the roof down on us all.

WRITER: This house is full of people.

MRS. WIRE: People I let rooms to. Less than strangers to me.

WRITER: There's—me. I'm not.

MRS. WIRE: You—just endure my company 'cause you're employed here, boy.

WRITER: Miss Sparks isn't employed here.

MRS. WIRE: That woman is close to no one but the bum she keeps here. I'll show you. [*She rises and knocks her chair over, then bawls out as if to Tye.*] More boxes! Take 'em out an' stay out with 'em, sleep it off on the streets!

[*Jane rises in her dim spot of light. She crosses to the door.*]

JANE [*offstage*]: Tye! Tye! I thought I heard Tye down there.

MRS. WIRE: Miss Sparks—don't you know that bum don't quit work till daybreak and rarely shows here before noon?

JANE: Sorry. Excuse me.

WRITER [*his speech slurred by drink*]: God, but I was ignorant when I came here! This place has been a—I ought to pay you—tuition . . .

MRS. WIRE: One drink has made you drunk, boy. Go up to bed. We're goin' on tomorrow like nothing happened. [*He rises and crosses unsteadily from the kitchen light.*] Be careful on the steps.

WRITER [*pausing to look back at her*]: Good night, Mrs. Wire. [*He disappears.*]

MRS. WIRE: —It's true, people die of it . . .

[*On the hall stairs the writer meets Nightingale, who speaks before the writer enters his own cubicle.*]

NIGHTINGALE [*imitating the writer's testimony in night court*]: "I, uh, think it's unlikely a lady would do such a thing." [*He coughs.*] —A statement belonging in a glossary of deathless quotations. [*He coughs again.*] —Completely convinced me you really do have a future in the—literary—profession.

[*The light builds on Mrs. Wire, and she rises from the kitchen table and utters a piercing cry. Nursie appears.*]

NURSIE: Mizz Wire, what on earth is it? A bat?

MRS. WIRE: I just felt like screaming, and so I screamed! That's all . . .

[*The lights dim out.*]

INTERVAL

PART TWO

A spotlight focuses on the writer working at his dilapidated typewriter in his gabled room in the attic.

WRITER: Instinct, it must have been[*He starts typing.*] directed me here, to the Vieux Carré of New Orleans, down country as a—river flows no plan. I couldn't have consciously, deliberately, selected a better place than here to discover—to encounter—my true nature. *Exposition! Shit!*

[*He springs up and kicks at the worn, wobbly table. A lean, gangling young man, whose charming but irresponsible nature is apparent in his genial grin, appears at the entrance of the writer's cubicle.*]

SKY: Having trouble?

WRITER: Even the typewriter objected to those goddamn lines. The ribbon's stuck, won't reverse.

SKY: Let me look at it. [*He enters the cubicle.*] Oh, my name is Schuyler but they call me Sky.

WRITER: The owner of the knapsack with "SKY" printed on it, that was—that was deposited here last winter sometime?

SKY [*working on the typewriter*]: Right. Landlady won't surrender it to me for less than twenty-five bucks, which is more than I can pay. Yeah, you see—I'm a fugitive from—from legal wedlock in Tampa, Florida, with the prettiest little bitsy piece of it you ever did see. There, now the ribbon's reversing, it slipped out of the slots like I slipped out of matrimony in Tampa—couldn't you see that?

69

WRITER: I don't think there's a room in this building where you could be certain it was night or day, and I've . . .

SKY: Something wrong with that eye.

WRITER: Operation. For a cataract. Just waiting till it heals.—Are you staying here?

SKY: Just for a day or two while I look into spots for a jazz musician in the Quarter.

WRITER: There's several jazz combos just around the corner on Bourbon Street.

SKY: Yeah, I know, but they're black and not anxious to work with a honky. So, I'll probably drive on West.

WRITER: How far West?

SKY: The Coast. Is there a toilet up here? I gotta piss. Downstairs john's occupied.

WRITER: I know a girl across the hall with a bathroom, but she's probably sleeping.

SKY: With the angels wetting the roof, would it matter if I did, too?

WRITER: Go ahead.

[*Sky leaps onto the alcove and pisses upstage out of the window.*]

Why'd you decide not to marry?

SKY: Suddenly realized I wasn't ready to settle. The girl, she had a passion for pink, but she extended it out of bounds in the love nest she'd picked out for us. Pink, pink, pink. So I cut out before daybreak.

WRITER: Without a word to the girl?

SKY: A note, "Not ready. Be back." Wonder if she believed it, or if I did. That was Christmas week. I asked permission to leave my knapsack here with the landlady, overnight. She said, "For fifty cents." Extortionary, but I accepted the deal. However was unavoidably detained like they say. Returned last night for my gear and goddam, this landlady here refuses to surrender it to me except for twenty-five bucks. Crazy witch!

[*Mrs. Wire is at the cubicle entrance.*]

MRS. WIRE: What's he doin' up there?

SKY: Admiring the view.

MRS. WIRE: You was urinating out of the window! Jailbird! You ain't been in a hospital four months, you been in the House of Detention for resistin' arrest and assaultin' an officer of the law. I know. You admire the view in the bathroom. I don't allow no trashy behavior here. [*She turns to the writer.*] Why ain't you on the streets with those business cards?

WRITER: Because I'm at the last paragraph of a story.

MRS. WIRE: Knock it off this minute! Why, the streets are swarming this Sunday with the Azalea Festival trade.

WRITER: The time I give to "Meals for a Quarter in the Quarter" has begun to exceed the time originally agreed on, Mrs. Wire.

71

MRS. WIRE: It's decent, healthy work that can keep you off bad habits, bad company that I know you been drifting into.

WRITER: How would you know anything outside of this moldy, old—

MRS. WIRE: Don't talk that way about this—*historical* old building. Why, 722 Toulouse Street is one of the oldest buildings in the Vieux Carré, and the courtyard, why, that courtyard out there is on the tourist list of attractions!

WRITER: The tourists don't hear you shoutin' orders and insults to your, your—prisoners here!

MRS. WIRE: Two worthless dependents on me, that pair of scavenger crones that creep about after dark.

[*Nightingale coughs in his cubicle. Mrs. Wire raises her voice.*]

And I got that TB case spitting contagion wherever he goes, leaves a track of blood behind him like a chicken that's had it's head chopped off.

NIGHTINGALE: 'sa goddam libelous lie!

MRS. WIRE [*crossing to the entrance of the adjoining cubicle*]: Been discharged from the Two Parrots, they told you to fold up your easel and git out!

NIGHTINGALE [*hoarsely*]: I'm making notes on these lies, and my friend, the writer, is witness to them!

MRS. WIRE: You is been discharged from the Two Parrots. It's God's truth, I got it from the cashier!

72

[*Sky chuckles, fascinated. He sits on the edge of the table or cot, taking a cigarette and offering one to the writer. Their casual friendly talk is contrapuntal to the violent altercation in progress outside.*]

She told me they had to scrub the pavement around your easel with a bucket of lye each night, that customers had left without payin' because you'd hawked an' spit by their tables!

NIGHTINGALE: Bucket of lies, not lye, that's what she told you!

MRS. WIRE: They only kept you there out of human pity!

NIGHTINGALE: Pity!

MRS. WIRE: Yais, pity! But finally pity and patience was exhausted, it run out there and it's run out here! Unlock that door! NURSIE!

NURSIE [*off stage*]: Now what?

MRS. WIRE: Bring up my keys! Mr. Nightingale's locked himself in! You're gonna find you'self mighty quicker than you expected in a charity ward on your way to a pauper's grave!

WRITER: Mrs. Wire, be easy on him . . .

MRS. WIRE: You ain't heard what he calls me? Why, things he's said to me I hate to repeat. He's called me a fuckin' ole witch, yes, because I stop him from bringin' pickups in here at midnight that might stick a knife in the heart of anyone in the buildin' after they done it to him.

NIGHTINGALE [*in a wheezing voice as he drops onto the cot in his cubicle*]: It's you that'll get a knife stuck in you, between your—dried up old—dugs . . .

73

WRITER [sotto voce, *near tears*]: Be easy on him, he's dying.

MRS. WIRE: Not here. He's defamed this place as infested with bedbugs to try to explain away the blood he coughs on his pillow.

WRITER: That's—his last defense against—

MRS. WIRE: The truth, there's no defense against truth. Ev'rything in that room is contaminated, has got to be removed to the incinerator an' burned. Start with the mattress, Nursie!

[*Nursie has entered the lighted area with a bunch of musty keys.*]

NIGHTINGALE: I warn you, if you attempt to enter my room, I'll strike you down with this easel!

MRS. WIRE: You do that, just try, the effort of the exertion would finish you right here! Oh, shoot, here's the master key, opens all doors!

NIGHTINGALE: At your own risk—I'll brain you, you bitch.

MRS. WIRE: Go on in there, Nursie!

NURSIE: Aw, no, not me! I told you I would never go in that room!

MRS. WIRE: We're coming in!

NIGHTINGALE: WATCH OUT!

[*He is backed into the alcove, the easel held over his head like a crucifix to exorcise a demon. A spasm of coughing wracks him. He bends double, dropping the easel, collapses to his knees, and then falls flat upon the floor.*]

NURSIE [*awed*]: Is he daid, Mizz Wire?

MRS. WIRE: Don't touch him. Leave him there until the coroner gets here.

NIGHTINGALE [*gasping*]: Coroner, your ass—I'll outlive you.

MRS. WIRE: If I dropped dead this second! Nursie, haul out that filthy mattress of his, pour kerosene on it.

NURSIE: Wouldn't touch that mattress with a pole . . .

MRS. WIRE: And burn it. Git a nigger to help you haul everything in here out, it's all contaminated. Why, this whole place could be quarantined!

NURSIE: Furniture?

MRS. WIRE: All! Then wash off your hands in alcohol to prevent infection, Nursie.

NURSIE: Mizz Wire, the courtyard is full of them Azalea Festival ladies that paid admission to enter! You want me to smoke 'em out?

MRS. WIRE: Collect the stuff you can move.

NURSIE: Move where?

MRS. WIRE: Pile it under the banana tree in the courtyard, cover it with tarpaulin, we can burn it later.

NIGHTINGALE: If anyone lays a hand on my personal effects,

I'll [*His voice chokes with sobs.*]—I will be back in the Two Parrots tonight. I wasn't fired. I was given a leave of absence till I recovered from . . . asthma . . .

MRS. WIRE [*with an abrupt compassion*]: Mr. Nightingale.

NIGHTINGALE: Rossignol!—of the Baton Rouge Rossignols, as any dog could tell you . . .

MRS. WIRE: I won't consult a dawg on this subject. However, the place for you is not here but in the charity ward at St. Vincent's. Rest there till I've made arrangements to remove you.

SKY: The altercation's subsided.

WRITER [*to Sky, who has begun to play his clarinet*]: What kind of horn is that?

[*Mrs. Wire appears at the entrance to the writer's cubicle. Sky plays entrance music—"Ta-ta-taaaa!"*]

SKY: It's not a horn, kid, horns are brass. A clarinet's a wood-wind instrument, not a horn.

MRS. WIRE: Yais, now about you all.

SKY: Never mind about us. We're leaving for the West Coast.

[*Mrs. Wire and the writer are equally stunned in opposite ways.*]

MRS. WIRE: —What's he mean, son? You're leavin' with this jailbird?

WRITER: —I—

MRS. WIRE: You won't if I can prevent it, and I know how. In my register book, when you signed in here, you wrote St. Louis. We got your home address, street and number. I'm gonna inform your folks of the vicious ways and companions you been slipping into. They's a shockin' diff'rence between your looks an' manners since when you arrived here an' now, mockin' me with that grin an' that shifty-eyed indifference, evidence you're setting out on a future life of corruption. Address and phone number, I'll write, I'll phone! —You're not leavin' here with a piece of trash like *that* that pissed out the window! —Son, son, don't do it! [*She covers her face, unraveled with emotion. Exchanging a look with Sky, the writer places an arm gingerly about her shoulder.*] You know I've sort of adopted you like the son took away from me by the late Mr. Wire and a—and a crooked lawyer, they got me declared to be—mentally incompetent.

WRITER: Mrs. Wire, I didn't escape from one mother to look for another.

[*Nursie returns, huffing, to the lighted area.*]

NURSIE: Mizz Wire, those tourists ladies, I can't control them, they're pickin' the azaleas off the bushes, and—

MRS. WIRE: That's what I told you to stay in the courtyard to stop.

NURSIE: Oh, I try, but one of 'em jus' called me a impudent ole nigger, and I won't take it. I come here to tell you I QUIT!

MRS. WIRE: AGAIN! COME BACK OUT THERE WITH ME! [*She turns to the writer.*] We'll continue this later. [*She exits with Nursie.*]

WRITER [*to Sky*]: —Were you serious about the West Coast offer?

SKY: You're welcome to come along with me. I don't like to travel a long distance like that by myself.

WRITER: How do you travel?

SKY: I've got a beat-up old '32 Ford across the street with a little oil and about half a tank of gas in it. If you want to go, we could share the expense. Have you got any cash?

WRITER: I guess I've accumulated a capital of about thirty-five dollars.

SKY: We'll siphon gas on the way.

WRITER: Siphon?

SKY: I travel with a little rubber tube, and at night I unscrew the top of somebody's gas tank and suck the gas out through the tube and spit it into a bucket and empty it into my car. Is it a deal?

WRITER [*with suppressed excitement*]: How would we live on the road?

SKY [*rolling a cigarette with obvious practice*]: We'd have to exercise our wits. And our personal charm. And, well, if that don't suffice, I have a blanket in the car, and there's plenty of wide open spaces between here and the Coast. [*He pauses for a beat.*] Scared? Of the undertaking?

WRITER [*smiling slowly*]: No—the Coast—starting when?

SKY: Why not this evening? The landlady won't admit me to the house again, but I'll call you. Just keep your window open. I'll blow my clarinet in the courtyard. Let's say about six.

[*The conversation may continue in undertones as the area is dimmed out.*]

The lights come up on Jane's studio area. The shuttered doors to the windows overlooking the courtyard below are ajar. Jane is trying to rouse Tye from an unnaturally deep sleep. It is evident that she has been engaged in packing her effects and his.

JANE: Tye, Tye, oh—Christ . . .

[*He drops a bare arm off the disordered bed and moans slightly. She bends over to examine a needle mark on his arm.*]

TYE: —Wh—?

[*Jane crosses to the sink and wets a towel, then returns to slap Tye's face with it. He begins to wake slowly.*]

Some men would beat a chick up for less'n that, y'know.

JANE: All right, get out of bed and beat me up, but get *up*.

TYE [*stroking a promontory beneath the bed sheet*]: —Can't you see I *am* up?

JANE: I don't mean that kind of up, and don't bring stripshow lewdness in here this—Sunday afternoon.

TYE: Babe, don't mention the show to me t'day.

JANE: I'd like to remind you that when we first stumbled into this—crazy—co-habitation, you promised me you'd quit the show in a week.

TYE: For what? Tight as work is for a dude with five grades of school and no skill training from the Mississippi sticks?

JANE: You could find something less—publicly embarrassing, like a—filling station attendant.

TYE: Ha!

JANE: But of course your choice of employment is no concern of mine now.

TYE: Why not, Babe?

JANE: I'm not "Babe" and not "Chick"!

TYE: You say you're not my chick?

JANE: I say I'm nobody's chick.

TYE: Any chick who shacks with me's my chick.

JANE: This is my place. You just—moved in and stayed.

TYE: I paid the rent this month.

JANE: Half of it, for the first time, my savings being as close to exhaustion as me.

[*There is the sound of a funky piano and a voice on the Bourbon Street corner: "I've stayed around and played around this old town too long." Jane's mood softens under its influence.*]

Lord, I don't know how I managed to haul you to bed.

TYE: Hey, you put me to bed last night?

JANE: It was much too much exertion for someone in my— condition.

TYE [*focusing on her more closely*]: —Honey, are you pregnant?

JANE: No, Lord, now who'd be fool enough to get pregnant by a Bourbon Street stripshow barker?

TYE: When a chick talks about her condition, don't it mean she's pregnant?

JANE: All female conditions are not pregnancy, Tye. [*She staggers, then finishes her coffee.*] Mine is that of a desperate young woman living with a young bum employed by gangsters and using her place as a depository for hot merchandise. Well, they're all packed. You're packed too.

TYE: —Come to bed.

JANE: No, thank you. Your face is smeared with lipstick; also other parts of you. I didn't know lip rouge ever covered so much—territory.

TYE: I honestly don't remember a fuckin' thing after midnight.

JANE: That I do believe. Now have some coffee, I've warmed it. It isn't instant, it's percolated.

TYE: Who's birthday is it?

JANE: It's percolated in honor of our day of parting.

TYE: Aw, be sweet, Babe, please come back to bed. I need comfort, not coffee.

JANE: You broke a promise to me.

TYE: Which?

81

JANE: Among the many? You used a needle last night. I saw the mark of it on you.

TYE: No shit. Where?

JANE [*returning to the bedside*]: There, right there on your— [*He circles her with his arm and pulls her onto the bed.*] I've been betrayed by a—sensual streak in my nature. Susceptibility to touch. And you have skin like a child. I'd gladly support you if I believed you'd—if I had the means to and the time to. Time. Means. Luck. Things that expire, run out. And all at once you're stranded.

TYE: Jane you—lie down with me and hold me.

JANE: I'm afraid, Tye, we'll just have to hold each other in our memories from now on.

TYE [*childishly*]: Don't talk that way. I never had a rougher night in my life. Do I have to think and remember?

JANE: Tye, we've had a long spell of dreaming, but now we suddenly have to.

TYE: Got any aspirin, Babe?

JANE: You're past aspirin, Tye. I think you've gone past all legal—analgesics.

TYE: You say words to me I've never heard before.

JANE: Tye, I've been forced to make an urgent phone call to someone I never wanted to call.

TYE: Call?

JANE: And then I packed your personal belongings and all that loot you've been holding here. Exertion of packing nearly blacked me out. Trembling, sweating—had to bathe and change.

TYE: Babe?

JANE: You're vacating the premises, "Babe." It's *afternoon*.

TYE: Look, if you're knocked up, have the kid. I'm against abortion.

JANE: On moral principles?

TYE: Have the kid, Babe. I'd pull myself together for a kid.

JANE: You didn't for me.

TYE: A baby would be a livin' thing between us, with both our blood.

JANE: Never mind.

[*Voices in the courtyard are heard.*]

NURSIE: Any donations t'keep the cou'tyard up, just drop it in my apron as you go out, ladies! . . .

JANE: Those tourists down there in the courtyard! If I'd known when I took this room it was over a tourist attraction—

TYE: It's the Festival, Babe. It ain't always Festival . . . gimme my cigarettes, ought to be some left in a pocket.

JANE [*throwing his pants and a fancy sport shirt on the bed*]: Here, your clothes, get in them.

83

TYE [*putting on his shorts*]: Not yet. It's Sunday, Babe . . . Where's Beret? I like Beret to be here when I wake up.

JANE: Not even a cat will wait ten, twelve hours for you to sleep off whatever you shot last night. How did a girl well educated and reasonably well brought up get involved in this . . . Oh, I'm talking to myself.

TYE: I hear you, Babe, and I see you.

JANE: Then . . . get up and dressed.

TYE: It's not dark yet, Babe. Y'know I never get dressed till after dark on Sundays.

JANE: Today has to be an exception. I'm . . . expecting a caller, very important to me.

TYE: Fashion designer?

JANE: No. Buyer . . . to look at my illustrations. They're no good, I'm no good. I just had a flair, not a talent, and the flair flared out, I'm . . . finished. These sketches are evidence of it! [*She starts tearing fashion sketches off the wall.*] Look at me! Bangles, jangles! All taste gone! [*She tears off her costume jewelry.*]

TYE: Babe, you're in no shape to meet a buyer.

JANE [*slowly and bitterly*]: He's no buyer of anything but me.

TYE: —Buyer of *you?* Look. You said that you were expecting a buyer to look at your drawin's here.

JANE: I know what I said, I said a buyer to look at my illus-

84

trations, but what I said was a lie. Among other things, many other undreamed of before, you've taught me to practice deception.

VOICES OFFSTAGE: Edwina, Edwina, come see this dream of a little courtyard. Oh, my, yaiss, like a dream.

JANE: I know what I said, but let's say, Tye, that I experienced last week a somewhat less than triumphant encounter with the buyer of fashion illustrations at *Vogue Moderne*. In fact, it left me too shattered to carry my portfolio home without a shot of Metaxas brandy at the Blue Lantern, which was on the street level of the building. It was there that I met a gentleman from Brazil. He had observed my entrance, the Brazilian, and apparently took me for a hooker, sprang up with surprising agility for a gentleman of his corpulence, hauled me to his table, and introduced me to his *camaradas*, "Señorita, this is Señor and Señor and Señor," declared me, "*Bonita, muy, muy, bonita*"— tried to press a hundred-dollar bill in my hand. Well, some atavistic bit of propriety surfaced and I, like a fool, rejected it—but did accept his business card, just in case. This morning, Tye, I called him. "Señorita Bonita of the Blue Lantern awaits you, top floor of seven-two-two Toulouse," that was the invitation that I phoned in to the message desk. He must have received it by now at the Hotel Royal Orleans, where the Presidential Suite somehow contains him.

TYE: Who're you talkin' about?

JANE: My expected caller, a responsible businessman from Brazil. Sincerely interested in my bankrupt state . . .

TYE: Forget it, come back to bed and I'll undress you, Babe, you need rest.

JANE: The bed bit is finished between us. You're moving out today.

85

[*He slowly stumbles up, crosses to the table, and gulps coffee, then grasps her arm and draws her to bed.*]

No, no, no, no, no, no!

TYE: Yes, yes, yes, yes, yes!

[*He throws her onto the bed and starts to strip her; she resists; he prevails. As the lights very gradually dim, a Negro singer-pianist at a nearby bar fades in, "Fly a-way! Sweet Kentucky baby-bay, fly, away . . ."*]

MRS. WIRE [*from a few steps below the writer*]: What's paralyzed you there? Son?

WRITER: Miss Sparks is crying.

[*Mrs. Wire appears behind the writer in the lighted spot.*]

MRS. WIRE: That woman's moanin' in there don't mean she's in pain. Son, I got a suspicion you never had close relations with wimmen in your life.

JANE: Ohhh!

WRITER: I never heard sounds like that.

[*Jane utters a wild cry. It impresses even Mrs. Wire.*]

TYE'S VOICE: Babe, I don't wanna force you . . .

JANE'S VOICE: Plee-ase! I'm not a thing, I'm not—a—thing!

MRS. WIRE [*shouting*]: You all quit that loud fornication in there!

86

TYE'S VOICE [*shouting back*]: Get the fuck downstairs, goddam ole witch!

MRS. WIRE: Howlin' insults at me in my own house, won't tolerate it! [*She bursts into the room.*] Never seen such a disgustin' exhibition!

[*Tye starts to rise from the bed. Jane clings desperately to him.*]

JANE: As! You see!—Mrs. Wire!—Everything is!—packed, he's —moving—today . . .

TYE: The rent is paid in full! So get the fuck outa here!

JANE: Tye, please.

MRS. WIRE: What's in them boxes?

TYE: None of your—

JANE: Our personal—belongings, Mrs. Wire.

MRS. WIRE: That I doubt! The contents of these boxes will be inspected before removed from this place and in the presence of my nephew on the police force!

[*Tye charges toward Mrs. Wire.*]

Don't you expose yourself naykid in my presence! Nursie!

JANE: Mrs. Wire, for once I do agree with you! Can you get him out, please, please get him out!

MRS. WIRE [*averting her face with an air of shocked propriety*]: Dress at once and—

87

NURSIE: Mizz Wire, I got the hospital on the phone.

MRS. WIRE: They sendin' an ambulance for Nightingale?

NURSIE: Soon's they got a bed for him, but they want you to call 'em back and—

MRS. WIRE: St. Vincent's is run by taxpayers' money, I'll remind 'em of that. [*She crosses off stage. Tye slams the door.*]

[*Jane is sobbing on the bed.*]

TYE: Now, Babe.

JANE: If you approach this bed—

TYE: Just want to comfort you, honey. Can't we just rest together? Can't we? Rest and comfort each other?

[*The area dims as the black pianist sings "Kentucky Baby."*]

MRS. WIRE: Cut out that obscene talking up there, I'm on the phone. Emergency call is from here at 722 Toulouse. Christ Almighty, you drive me to profane language. You mean to admit you don't know the location of the most historical street in the Vieux Carré? You're not talking to no . . . no nobody, but a personage. Responsible. Reputable. Known to the authorities on the list of attractions. God damn it, you twist my tongue up with your . . . Nursie! Nursie! Will you talk to this incompetent . . . Nursie! Nursie!

[*Nursie appears.*]

Got some idiot on the phone at the hospital. Will you inform this idiot who I am in the Quarter. Phone. Talk.

[*Nursie takes the phone.*]

NURSIE: Stairs . . . took my breath . . .

MRS. WIRE [*snatching back the phone*]: Now I want you to
know, this here Nightingale case . . . I don't lack sympathy for
the dying or the hopelessly inflicted . . . [*She kicks at Nursie
beside her.*] Git! But I've got responsibilities to my tenants.
Valuable paying tenants, distinguished society ladies, will quit
my premises this day, I swear they will, if this Nightingale remains. Why, the State Board of Health will clap a suit on me
unless . . . at once . . . ambulance. When? At what time?
Don't say approximate to me. Emergency means immediate. Not
when you drag your arse around to it. And just you remember
I'm a taxpayer . . . No, no, you not me. I pay, you collect.
Now get the ambulance here immediately, 722 Toulouse, with a
stretcher with straps, the Nightingale is violent with fever. [*She
slams down the phone.*] Shit!

NURSIE: My guess is they're going to remove you, too. ✓

[*Mrs. Wire leans on Nursie.*]

There is a spotlight on the writer, stage front, as narrator.

WRITER: That Sunday I served my last meal for a quarter in the Quarter, then I returned to the attic. From Nightingale's cage there was silence so complete I thought, "He's dead." Then he cried out softly—

NIGHTINGALE: Christ, how long do I have to go on like this?

WRITER: Then, for the first time, I returned his visits. [*He makes the gesture of knocking at Nightingale's door.*]—Mr. Rossignol . . .

[*There is a sound of staggering and wheezing. Nightingale opens the door; the writer catches him as he nearly falls and assists him back to his cot.*]

—You shouldn't try to dress.

NIGHTINGALE: Got to—escape! She wants to commit me to a charnal house on false charges . . .

WRITER: It's raining out.

NIGHTINGALE: A Rossignol will not be hauled away to a charity hospital.

WRITER: Let me call a private doctor. He wouldn't allow them to move you in your—condition . . .

NIGHTINGALE: My faith's in Christ—not doctors . . .

WRITER: Lie down.

NIGHTINGALE: Can't breathe lying—down . . .

WRITER: I've brought you this pillow. I'll put it back of your head. [*He places the pillow gently in back of Nightingale.*] Two plilows help you breathe.

NIGHTINGALE [*leaning weakly back*]: Ah—thanks—better . . . Sit down.

[*A dim light comes up on the studio area as Tye, sitting on the table, lights a joint.*]

WRITER: Theren' nowhere to sit.

NIGHTINGALE: You mean nowhere not contaminated? [*The writer sits.*] —God's got to give me time for serious work! Even God has moral obligations, don't He? —Well, *don't* He?

WRITER: I think that morals are a human invention that He ignores as successfully as we do.

NIGHTINGALE: Christ, that's evil, that is infidel talk. [*He crosses himself.*] I'm a Cath'lic believer. A priest would say that you have fallen from Grace, boy.

WRITER: What's that you're holding?

NIGHTINGALE: Articles left me by my sainted mother. Her tortoise-shell comb with a mother-of-pearl handle and her silver framed mirror.

[*He sits up with difficulty and starts combing his hair before the mirror as if preparing for a social appearance.*]

Precious heirlooms, been in the Rossignol family three generations. I look pale from confinement with asthma. Bottom of box is—toiletries, cosmetics—please!

WRITER: You're planning to make a public appearance, intending to go on the streets with this—advanced case of asthma?

NIGHTINGALE: Would you kindly hand me my Max Factor, my makeup kit?!

WRITER: I have a friend who wears cosmetics at night—they dissolve in the rain.

NIGHTINGALE: If necessary, I'll go into *Sanctuary!*

[*The writer utters a startled, helpless laugh; he shakes with it and leans against the stippled wall.*]

Joke, is it, is it a joke?! Foxes have holes, but the Son of Man hath nowhere to hide His head!

WRITER: Don't you know you're delirious with fever?

NIGHTINGALE: You used to be kind—gentle. In less than four months you've turned your back on that side of your nature, turned rock-hard as the world.

WRITER: I had to survive in the world. Now where's your pills for sleep, you need to rest.

NIGHTINGALE: On the chair by the bed.

[*Pause.*]

WRITER [*softly*]: Maybe this time you ought to take more than one.

NIGHTINGALE: Why, you're suggesting suicide to me which is a cardinal sin, would put me in unhallowed ground in—potter's field. I believe in God the Father, God the Son, and God the Holy Ghost . . . you've turned into a killer?

WRITER [*compulsively, with difficulty*]: Stop calling it asthma —the flu, a bad cold. Face the facts, deal with them. [*He opens the pillbox.*] Press tab to open, push down, unscrew the top. Here it is where you can reach it.

NIGHTINGALE: —Boy with soft skin and stone heart . . .

[*Pause. The writer blows the candle out and takes Nightingale's hand.*]

WRITER: Hear the rain, let the rain talk to you, I can't.

NIGHTINGALE: Light the candle.

WRITER: The candle's not necessary. You've got an alcove, too, with a window and bench. Keep your eyes on it, she might come in here before you fall asleep.

[*A strain of music is heard. The angel enters from her dark passage and seats herself, just visible faintly, on Nightingale's alcove bench.*]

Do you see her in the alcove?

NIGHTINGALE: Who?

WRITER: Do you feel a comforting presence?

NIGHTINGALE: None.

WRITER: Remember my mother's mother? Grand?

NIGHTINGALE: I don't receive apparitions. They're only seen by the mad.

[*The writer returns to his cubicle and continues as narrator.*]

WRITER: In my own cubicle, I wasn't sure if Grand had entered with me or not. I couldn't distinguish her from a—diffusion of light through the low running clouds. I thought I saw her, but her image was much fainter than it had ever been before, and I suspected that it would fade more and more as the storm of my father's blood obliterated the tenderness of Grand's. I began to pack my belongings. I was about to make a panicky departure to nowhere I could imagine . . . The West Coast? With Sky?

[*He is throwing things into a cardboard suitcase. Nursie appears at the edge of his light with a coffee tray.*]

NURSIE: Mizz Wire knows you're packin' to leave an' she tole me to bring you up this hot coffee and cold biscuits.

WRITER: Thank her. Thank you both.

NURSIE: She says don't make no mistakes.

WRITER [*harshly*]: None, never?

NURSIE: None if you can help, and I agree with her about that. She's phoned your folks about you. They're coming down here tomorrow.

WRITER: If she's not bluffing . . .

NURSIE: She ain't bluffin', I heard her on the phone myself. Mizz Wire is gettin' you confused with her son Timmy. Her mind is slippin' again. Been through that before. Can't do it again.

WRITER: We all have our confusions . . . [*He gulps down the coffee as Nursie crosses out of the light.*]

NURSIE [*singing softly*]: "My home is on Jordan."

WRITER: Then I started to write. I worked the longest I'd ever worked in my life, nearly all that Sunday. I wrote about Jane and Tye, I could hear them across the narrow hall. —Writers are shameless spies . . .

The studio light builds. Jane is sobbing on the bed. Tye is rolling a joint, seated on the table. The clearing sky has faded toward early blue dusk. Tye regards Jane with a puzzled look. Faintly we hear the black singer-pianist. "Bye, bye, blues. Don't cry blues," etc.

TYE: Want a hit, Babe? [*She ignores the question.*] How long have I been asleep? Christ, what are you crying about. Didn't I just give you one helluva Sunday afternoon ball, and you're cryin' about it like your mother died.

JANE: You forced me, you little pig, you did, you forced me.

TYE: You wanted it.

JANE: I didn't.

TYE: Sure you did. [*Jane is dressing again.*] Honey, you got shadows under your eyes.

JANE: Blackbirds kissed me last night. Isn't that what they say about shadows under the eyes, that blackbirds kissed her last night. The Brazilian must have been blind drunk when he took a fancy to me in the Blue Lantern, mistook me for a hundred-dollar girl. —Tye, I'm not a whore! I'm the Northern equivalent of a lady, fallen, yes, but a lady, not a whore.

TYE: Whores get paid for it, Babe. I never had to.

JANE: You little—prick! Now I'm talkin' your jive, how do you like it? Does she talk like that when she's smearing you with lipstick, when you ball her, which I know you do, repeatedly, between shows.

96

TYE: —Who're you talkin' about?

JANE: That headliner at the strip show, the Champagne Girl.

TYE [*gravely*]: She's—not with the show no more.

JANE: The headliner's quit the show?

TYE: Yeah, honey, the Champagne Girl is dead an' so she's not in the show.

JANE: You mean—not such a hot attraction any more?

TYE: Don't be funny about it, it ain't funny.

JANE: You mean she's actually—

TYE: Yes. Ackshally. Dead. Real dead, about as dead as dead, which is totally dead— So now you know why I needed a needle to get me through last night.

JANE: —Well, of course that's—

TYE: You was jealous of her . . . [*Jane looks away.*] I never touched the Champagne Girl. She was strictly the property of the Man. Nobody else dared t' touch her.

JANE: The Man—what man?

TYE: The Man—no other name known by. —Well—he wasted her.

JANE: —Killed her? —Why?

TYE: 'Cause she quit sleeping with him. She was offered a deal on the West Coast, Babe. The Man said, "No." The Champagne

97

Girl said, "Yes." So the Man . . . you don't say no to the Man—
so if she's going to the West Coast it'll be packed in ice—

[*Voices are heard from the courtyard.*]

TOURIST 1: My slippers are wet through.

[*Piano music is heard.*]

TOURIST 2: What's next on the tour, or is it nearly finished?

TYE: When the Man is annoyed by something, he piles his
lupos in the back seat of his bulletproof limo and he let's 'em
loose on the source of his annoyance.

JANE: —Lupos?

TYE: Lupos are those big black dawgs that're used for attack.
The Man has three of 'em, and when he patrols his territory at
night, they sit in the back seat of his Lincoln, set up there,
mouths wide open on their dagger teeth and their black eyes
rollin' like dice in a nigger crapshooter's hands. And night before
last, Jesus! he let 'em into the Champagne Girl's apartment, and
they—well, they ate her. Gnawed her tits off her ribs, gnawed
her sweet little ass off. Of course the story is that the Champagne
Girl entertained a pervert who killed her and ate her like that,
but it's pretty well known it was them lupos that devoured that
girl, under those ceiling mirrors and crystal chandeliers in her
all white satin bedroom. —Yep—gone—the headliner— Y'know
what you say when the Man wastes somebody? You got to say
that he or she has "Gone to Spain." So they tole me last night,
when people ask you where's the Champagne Girl, answer 'em
that the Champagne Girl's gone to Spain. —Sweet kid from
Pascagoula.

JANE: Please don't—continue—the story.

TYE: All champagne colored without face or body makeup on her, light gold like pale champagne and not a line, not a pore to be seen on her body! Was she meant for dawg food? I said, was she meant for dawg food? Those lupos ate that kid like she was their—last—supper . . .

JANE [*who has now managed to get round the table*]: Tye, Tye, open the shutters!

TYE: Why? You goin' out naked?

JANE: I'm going to vomit and die—in clean air, . . . [*She has moved slowly upstage to the gallery with its closed shutters, moving from one piece of furniture to another for support. Now she opens the shutter doors and staggers out onto the gallery, and the tourist ladies' voices are raised in thrilled shock and dismay.*]

TOURIST 1: Look at that!

TOURIST 2: What at?

TOURIST 1: There's a whore at the gallery window! Practically naked!

[*All gallery speeches should overlap.*]

JANE [*wildly*]: Out, out, out, out, out!

NURSIE: Miss, Miss Sparks! These are Festival ladies who've paid admission.

JANE: Can't endure any more! Please, please, I'm sick!

TYE: Fawgit it, Babe, come back in.

JANE: It isn't real, it couldn't be—

99

[*The writer shakes his head with a sad smile.*]

But it was—it is . . . like a dream . . .

TYE: What did you say, Babe?

JANE: Close the gallery door—please?

TYE: Sure, Babe. [*He shuts the door on the voices below.*]

JANE: And—the hall door—bolt it. Why do you bring home nightmare stories to me?!

TYE [*gently*]: Babe, you brought up the subject, you asked me about the Champagne Girl, I wasn't planning to tell you. Chair?

JANE: Bed.

TYE: Weed?

JANE: —Coffee.

TYE: Cold.

JANE: —Cold—coffee.

[*Tye pours her a cup and puts it in her trembling hand. He holds the hand and lifts the cup to her lips, standing behind her. He lets his hand fall to her breasts; she sobs and removes the hand.*

[*The singer-pianist is heard again.*]

JANE: . . . Why do you want to stay on here?

TYE: Here's where you are, Babe.

JANE [*shaking her head*]: No more. I . . . have to dress . . . [*She dresses awkwardly, frantically. He watches in silence.*] You have to get dressed, too. I told you I was expecting a very important visitor. Tye, the situation's turned impossible on us, face it.

TYE: You're not walkin' out on me.

JANE: Who have I got to appeal to except God, whose phone's disconnected, or this . . . providential . . . protector.

TYE: From the banana republic, a greaseball. And you'd quit me for that?

JANE: You've got to be mature and understanding. At least for once, now dress. The Brazilian is past due . . . I realized your defects, but you touched me like nobody else in my life had ever before or ever could again. But, Tye, I counted on you to grow up, and you refused to. I took you for someone gentle caught in violence and degradation that he'd escape from . . .

TYE: Whatever you took me for, I took you for honest, for decent, for . . .

JANE: Don't be so . . . "Decent"? You ridiculous little . . . sorry, no. Let's not go into . . . abuse . . . Tye? When we went into this it wasn't with any long-term thing in mind. That's him on the steps. Go in the bathroom quiet!

TYE: You go in the bathroom quiet. I'll explain without words.

[*She thrusts his clothes at him. He throws them savagely about the stage.*]

. . . Well?

[*There is a sound on the stairs.*]

Sounds like the footsteps of a responsible man.

[*Tye opens the door. We see hospital interns with a stretcher. Jane stares out. The interns pass again with Nightingale's dying body on the stretcher. The writer is with them. Jane gasps and covers her face with her arm. The writer turns to her.*]

WRITER: It's just—they're removing the painter.

JANE: —*Just!*

TYE: No Brazilian, no buyer?

JANE: No. No sale . . .

WRITER [*standing in the open doorway, as narrator*]: It was getting dim in the room.

TYE: It's almost getting dark.

WRITER: They didn't talk. He smoked his reefer. He looked at her steady in the room getting dark and said . . .

TYE: I see you clear.

WRITER: She turned her face away. He walked around that way and looked at her from that side. She turned her face the other way. She was crying without a sound, and a black man

102

was playing piano at the Four Deuces round the corner, an oldie, right for the atmosphere . . . something like . . .

[*The piano fades in, "Seem like Old Times." Tye begins to sing softly with the piano.*]

JANE: Don't.

[*Tye stops the soft singing but continues to stare at Jane.*]

DON'T

[*Pause.*]

TYE: Jane. You've gotten sort of—skinny. How much weight you lost?

JANE: I . . . don't know . . .

TYE: Sometimes you walk a block and can't go no further.

[*Pause.*]

JANE: I guess I'm a yellow-cab girl. With limousine aspirations.

TYE: Cut the smart talk, Babe. Let's level.

[*Pause. She extends her hand.*]

Want a drag? Well?

[*Jane nods and takes a drag off his cigarette.*]

Huh?

JANE: Well, after all, why not, if you're interested in it. It hasn't been just lately I've lost weight and energy but for more than a year in New York. Some—blood thing—progressing rather fast at my age . . . I think I had a remission when I met you. A definite remission . . . here . . . like the world stopped and turned backward, or like it entered another universe— *months!* [*She moves convulsively; Tye grips her shoulders.*] . . . Then . . . it . . . I . . .

TYE: Us?

JANE: No, no, that unnatural tiredness started in again. I went to Ochsners. Don't you remember when the doctor's letter was delivered? No, I guess you don't, being half conscious all the time. It was from Ochsners. It informed me that my blood count had changed for the worse. It was close to . . . collapse . . . [*Pause.*] . . . Those are the clinical details. Are you satisfied with them? Have you any more questions to ask?

[*She stares at him; he averts his face. She moves around him to look at his face; he averts it again. She claps it between her hands and compels him to look at her. He looks down. A scratching sound is heard at the shutter doors.*]

JANE: That's Beret, let her in. Isn't it nice how cats go away and come back and—you don't have to worry about them. So unlike human beings.

[*Tye opens the door. He opens a can of cat food and sets it on the floor, then crosses to his clothes, collecting them from the floor.*]

TYE [*gently*]: Jane, it's getting dark and I—I better get dressed now.

JANE [*with a touch of harshness*]: Yes, dress—dress . . . [*But he is lost in reflection, lighting a joint. She snatches it from his lips.*]

And leave me alone as always in a room that smells, that reeks of marijuana!

SCENE TWELVE

WRITER [*as narrator*]: She was watching him with an unspoken question in her eyes, a little resentful now.

MRS. WIRE'S VOICE [*from off stage, curiously altered*]: Why are those stairs so dark?

[*The light in the studio area is dimmed to half during the brief scene that follows. The writer rises and stands apprehensively alert as Mrs. Wire becomes visible in a yellowed silk robe with torn lace, a reliquary garment. Her hair is loose, her steps unsteady, her eyes hallucinated.*]

WRITER [*crossing from the studio, dismayed*]: Is that you, Mrs. Wire?

MRS. WIRE: Now, Timmy, Timmy, you mustn't cry every time Daddy gets home from the road and naturally wants to be in bed just with Mommy. It's Daddy's privilege, Mommy's—obligation. You'll understand when you're older—you see, Daddy finds Mommy attractive.

WRITER [*backing away from the cubicle entrance*]: Mrs. Wire, you're dreaming.

MRS. WIRE: Things between grownups in love and marriage can't be told to a child. [*She sits on the writer's cot.*] Now lie down and Mommy will sing you a little sleepy-time song. [*She is staring into space. He moves to the cubicle entrance; the candle is turned over and snuffed out.*]

MRS. WIRE: "Rock-a-bye, baby, in a tree top, If the wind blows, the cradle will rock . . ."

WRITER: Mrs. Wire, I'm not Timothy, I'm not Tim, I'm not Timmy. [*He touches her.*]

MRS. WIRE: Dear child given to me of love . . .

WRITER: Mrs. Wire, I'm not your child. I am nobody's child. Was maybe, but not now. I've grown into a man, about to take his first step out of this waiting station into the world.

MRS. WIRE: Mummy knows you're scared sleeping alone in the dark. But the Lord gave us dark for sleep, and Daddy don't like to find you took his rightful place . . .

WRITER: Mrs. Wire, I'm no relation to you, none but a tenant that earned his keep a while . . . Nursie! Nursie!

NURSIE [approaching]: She gone up there? [Nursie appears.] She gets these spells, goes back in time. I think it musta been all that Azalea Festival excitement done it.

MRS. WIRE: "If the bough breaks, the cradle will fall . . ."

NURSIE [at the cubicle entrance]: Mizz Wire, it's Nursie. I'll take you back downstairs.

MRS. WIRE [rousing a bit]: It all seemed so real. —I even remember lovemaking . . .

NURSIE: Get up, Mizz Wire, come down with Nursie.

MRS. WIRE [accepting Nursie's support]: Now I'm—old.

[They withdraw from the light.]

MRS. WIRE'S VOICE: Ahhhhhhhh . . . Ahhhhhhhh . . . Ahhhh . . . Ahhhhh . . .

[This expression of despair is lost in the murmur of the wind. The writer sinks onto his cot; the angel of the alcove appears in the dusk.]

107

WRITER: Grand! [*She lifts her hand in a valedictory gesture.*] I guess angels warn you to leave a place by leaving before you.

[*The light dims in the cubicle as the writer begins to pack and builds back up in the studio. The writer returns to the edge of the studio light.*]

JANE: You said you were going to get dressed and go back to your place of employment and resume the pitch for the ladies.

TYE: What did you say, Babe?

[*He has finished dressing and is now at the mirror, absorbed in combing his hair. Jane utters a soft, involuntary laugh.*]

JANE: A hundred dollars, the price, and worth it, certainly worth it. I must be much in your debt, way over my means to pay off!

TYE: Well, I ain't paid to make a bad appearance at work. [*He puts on a sport shirt with girls in grass skirts printed on it.*]

JANE: I hate that shirt.

TYE: I know you think it's tacky. Well, I'm tacky, and it's the only clean one I got.

JANE: It isn't clean, not really. And does it express much grief over the Champagne Girl's violent departure to Spain?

TYE: Do you have to hit me with that? What reason . . . ?

JANE: I've really got no reason to hit a goddamn soul but myself that lacked pride to keep my secrets. You know I shouldn't have told you about my—intentions, I should have just slipped

108

away. The Brazilian was far from attractive but—my circumstances required some drastic—compromises.

TYE [*crouching beside her*]: You're talking no sense, Jane. The Brazilian's out of the picture; those steps on the stairs were steps of hospital workers coming to take a—pick a dying fruit outa the place.

JANE: *Do you think I expect you back here again?* You'll say yes, assure me now as if forever—but—reconsider—the moment of impulse . . .

TYE: Cut some slack for me, Babe. We all gotta cut some slack for each other in this fucking world. Lissen. You don't have to sweat it.

JANE: Give me another remission; one that lasts!

TYE: Gotta go now, it's late, after dark and I'm dressed.

JANE: Well, zip your fly up unless you're now in the show. [*She rises and zips up his fly, touches his face and throat with trembling fingers.*]

TYE: Jane, we got love between us! Don't ya know that?

JANE [*not harshly*]: Lovely old word, love, it's travelled a long way, Tye.

TYE: And still's a long way to go. Hate to leave you alone, but—

JANE: I'm not alone. I've got Beret. An animal is a comforting presence sometimes. I wonder if they'd admit her to St. Vincent's?

109

TYE: St. Vincent's?

JANE: That charity hospital where they took the painter called Nightingale.

TYE: You ain't going there, honey.

JANE: It strikes me as being a likely destination.

TYE: Why?

JANE: I watched you dress. I didn't exist for you. Nothing existed for you but your image in the mirror. Understandably so. [*With her last strength she draws herself up.*]

TYE: What's understandable, Jane? —You got a fever? [*He rises, too, and stretches out a hand to touch her forehead. She knocks it away.*]

JANE: What's understandable is that your present convenience is about to become an encumbrance. An invalid, of no use, financial or sexual. Sickness is repellent, Tye, demands more care and gives less and less in return. The person you loved—assuming that you *did* love when she was still useful—is now, is now as absorbed in preparing herself for oblivion as you were absorbed, in your—your image in the—mirror!

TYE [*frightened by her vehemence*]: Hey, Jane!

[*Again she strikes away his extended hand.*]

JANE: Readies herself for it as you do for the street! [*She continues as to herself.*] —Withdraws into another dimension. Is indifferent to you except as—caretaker! Is less aware of you than of—[*Panting, she looks up slowly through the skylight.*]— sky that's visible to her from her bed under the skylight—at

110

night, these—filmy white clouds, they move, they drift over the roofs of the Vieux Carré so close that if you have fever you feel as if you could touch them, and bits would come off on your fingers, soft as—cotton candy—

TYE: Rest, Babe. I'll be back early. I'll get Smokey to take over for me at midnight, and I'll come back with tamales and a bottle of vino! [*He crosses out of the light. She rushes to the door.*]

JANE: *No, no, not before daybreak and with a new needle mark on your arm.* Beret? Beret!

[*She staggers wildly out of the light, calling the cat again and again.*]

WRITER: I lifted her from the floor where she'd fallen . . .

[*Various voices are heard exclaiming around the house.*

[*The writer reappears in the studio area supporting Jane, who appears half conscious.*]

Jane? Jane?

JANE: —My cat, I scared it away . . .

NURSIE [*offstage*]: What is goin' on up there?

WRITER: She was frightened by something.

JANE: I lost my cat, that's all. —They don't understand . . . [*The writer places her on the bed.*] Alone. I'm alone.

WRITER: She'll be back. [*He continues as narrator.*] Jane didn't seem to hear me. She was looking up at the skylight.

111

JANE: It isn't blue any more, it's suddenly turned quite dark.

WRITER: It was dark as the question in her eyes. [*The blues piano fades in.*]

JANE: It's black as the piano man playing around the corner.

WRITER [*to Jane*]: It must be after six. What's the time now?

JANE: Time? What? Oh. Time. My sight is blurred. [*She shows him her wristwatch.*] Can't make out the luminous dial, can you?

WRITER: It says five of twelve.

JANE: An improbable hour. Must have run down.

WRITER: I'll take it off. To wind it. [*He puts the watch to his ear.*] I'm afraid it's broken.

JANE [*vaguely*]: I hadn't noticed. —Lately— I tell time by the sky.

WRITER: His name was Sky.

JANE: Tye . . .

WRITER: No, not Tye. Sky was the name of someone who offered me a ride West.

JANE: —I've had fever all day. Did you ask me a question?

WRITER: I said I'd planned a trip to the West Coast with this young vagrant, a musician.

JANE: Young vagrants are irresponsible. I'm not at all surprised—he let you down? Well. I have travel plans, too.

112

WRITER: With Tye?

JANE: No, I was going alone, not with Tye. What are you doing there?

WRITER: Setting up the chess board. Want to play?

JANE: Oh, yes, you said you play. I'd have a partner for once. But my concentration's—I warn you—it's likely to be—impaired.

WRITER: Want to play white or black?

JANE: You choose.

[*The piano fades in. Jane looks about in a confused way.*]

WRITER: Black. In honor of the musician around the corner.

JANE: —He's playing something appropriate to the occasion as if I'd phoned in a request. How's it go, so familiar?

WRITER: "Makes no difference how things break,
    I'll still get by somehow
    I'm not sorry, cause it makes no difference now."

JANE: Each of us abandoned to the other. You know this is almost our first private conversation. [*She nearly falls to the floor. He catches her and supports her to the chair at the upstage side of the table.*] Shall we play, let's do. With no distractions at all. [*She seems unable to move; she has a frozen attitude.*]

[*There is a distant sustained high note from Sky's clarinet. They both hear it. Jane tries to distract the writer's attention from the sound and continues quickly with feverish animation. The sound of the clarinet becomes more urgent.*]

113

Vagrants, I can tell you about them. From experience. Incor-
irgibly delinquent. Purposeless. Addictive. Grab at you for support when support's what *you* need—gone? Whistling down the
last flight, such a lively popular tune. Well, I have travel plans,
but in the company of no charming young vagrant. Love Medi-
terranean countries but somehow missed Spain. I plan to go.
Now! Madrid, to visit the Prado, most celebrated museum of all.
Admire the Goyas, El Grecos. Hire a car to cross the—gold
plains of Toledo.

WRITER: Jane, you don't have to make up stories, I heard your
talk with Tye—all of it.

JANE: Then you must have heard his leaving. How his steps
picked up speed on the second flight down—started whistling . . .

WRITER: He always whistles down stairs—it's habitual to him—
you mustn't attach a special meaning to it.

[*The clarinet music is closer; the sound penetrates the shut
windows.*]

JANE: At night the Quarter's so full of jazz music, so many
entertainers. Isn't it now your move?

WRITER [*embarrassed*]: It's your move, Jane.

JANE [*relinquishing her game*]: No yours—your vagrant musician is late but you're not forgotten.

WRITER: I'll call down, ask him to wait till midnight when
Tye said he'll be back.

JANE: With tamales and vino to celebrate—[*She staggers to

the window, shatters a pane of glass, and shouts.] —Your friend's coming right down, just picking up his luggage!

[She leans against the wall, panting, her bleeding hand behind her.]

Now go, quick. He might not wait, you'd regret it.

WRITER: Can't I do something for you?

JANE: Pour me three fingers of bourbon.

[She has returned to the table. He pours the shot.]

Now hurry, hurry. I know that Tye will be back early tonight.

WRITER: Yes, of course he will . . . [He crosses from the studio light.]

JANE [smiling somewhat bitterly]: Naturally, yes, how could I possibly doubt it. With tamales and vino . . . [She uncloses her fist; the blood is running from palm to wrist. The writer picks up a cardboard laundry box and the typewriter case.]

WRITER: As I left, I glanced in Jane's door. She seemed to be or was pretending to be—absorbed in her solitary chess game. I went down the second flight and on the cot in the dark passageway was—[He calls out.] Beret?

[For the first time the cat is visible, white and fluffy as a piece of cloud. Nursie looms dimly behind him, a dark solemn fact, lamplit.]

NURSIE: It's the cat Miss Sparks come runnin' after.

WRITER: Take it to her, Nursie. She's alone up there.

MRS. WIRE: Now watch out, boy. Be careful of the future. It's a long ways for the young. Some makes it and others git lost.

WRITER: I know . . . [*He turns to the audience.*] I stood by the door uncertainly for a moment or two. I must have been frightened of it . . .

MRS. WIRE: Can you see the door?

WRITER: Yes—but to open it is a desperate undertaking . . . !

[*He does, hesitantly. Transparencies close from either wing. Dim spots of light touch each character of the play in a characteristic position.*

[*As he first draws the door open, he is forced back a few steps by a cacophony of sound: the waiting storm of his future—mechanical racking cries of pain and pleasure, snatches of song. It fades out. Again there is the urgent call of the clarinet. He crosses to the open door.*]

They're disappearing behind me. Going. People you've known in places do that: they go when you go. The earth seems to swallow them up, the walls absorb them like moisture, remain with you only as ghosts; their voices are echoes, fading but remembered.

[*The clarinet calls again. He turns for a moment at the door.*]

This house is empty now.

THE END